# The Passion of Perpetua

Marie-Louise von Franz, Honorary Patron

**Studies in Jungian Psychology
by Jungian Analysts**

Daryl Sharp, General Editor

# The Passion of Perpetua

## A Psychological Interpretation of Her Visions

**MARIE-LOUISE VON FRANZ**

**Edited by Daryl Sharp**

*See final pages for more titles in this series
by Marie-Louise von Franz and others*

**National Library of Canada Cataloguing in Publication Data**

Franz, Marie-Louise von, 1915-1998
    The passion of Perpetua: a psychological interpretation of
    her visions / Marie-Louise von Franz; edited by Daryl Sharp.

(Studies in Jungian psychology by Jungian analysts; 110)
Includes bibliographical references and index.

ISBN 1-894574-11-7

1. Perpetua, Saint, d. 203. 2. Dream interpretation.
3. Dreams—Religious aspects—Christianity. 4. Jungian psychology.
I. Sharp, Daryl, 1936-. II. Title. III. Series.

BR1720.P42F72 2004      154.6'3      C2003-907209-6

INNER CITY BOOKS
Box 1271, Station Q, Toronto, ON M4T 2P4, Canada
Telephone (416) 927-0355 / Fax (416) 924-1814
Web site: www.innercitybooks.net / E-mail: admin@innercitybooks.net

Honorary Patron: Marie-Louise von Franz.
Publisher and General Editor: Daryl Sharp.
Senior Editor: Victoria B. Cowan.

INNER CITY BOOKS was founded in 1980 to promote the
understanding and practical application of the work of C.G. Jung.

*Cover:* Color mosaic of St. Perpetua (Archbishop's palace, Ravenna, Italy).

Printed and bound in Canada by University of Toronto Press Incorporated

# CONTENTS

# Illustrations

# Editor's Foreword

The substance of this book, originally written in German and published in 1951 with C.G. Jung's *Aion*, is Marie-Louise von Franz's discussion and interpretation of the dreams—sometimes referred to as visions—of St. Perpetua, an African Christian martyred in 203 A.D. As Dr. von Franz notes in her introduction, her study grew out of a book report she undertook as a member of a seminar led by Jung.

This material was first published in an English translation by the late Elizabeth Welsh in the journal *Spring 1949*, under the title "The Passio Perpetua." In 1980 it was published by Spring Publications in its Jungian Classics Series. The text presented here is based on the 1980 Spring edition. I added the appendix, chose the illustrations and compiled the bibliography. Some references have been added or updated. The sources for some quoted material could not be found.

There are perhaps many readers who have never heard of St. Perpetua (patron saint of mothers in the Catholic pantheon), but who nevertheless have this book in hand because they appreciate the psychological understanding that Dr. von Franz brought to everything she focused on—alchemical texts, fairy tales, dreams, Jung's model of typology, and much, much more.

I think they will not be disappointed.

*Daryl Sharp*

# Marie-Louise von Franz, 1915-1998

Marie-Louise von Franz emigrated to Switzerland from Austria with her family in 1918. In 1933, at the age of 18, she attended a lecture by Professor C.G. Jung, then a mature 58. In his talk, Jung referred to a woman he had treated who "lived on the moon." The young Marie-Louise asked timorously if he meant that it was "as if" she lived on the moon. Jung replied, "No, not 'as if,' she *did* live on the moon."

This was von Franz's introduction to the reality of the unconscious. The very next year she began to work with Jung, first in analysis and then as his assistant in translating arcane alchemical texts, and did so until his death in 1961. In 1938 she was granted Swiss citizenship. In 1940 she received her doctorate in classical languages from the University of Zürich. In 1948 she was a co-founder, with Jung, of the C.G. Jung Institute of Zürich. Thereafter she lectured extensively and became internationally known as the doyenne of Jungian analysts, renowned for her work on synchronicity, dreams, alchemy and fairy tales.

# 1
# Introduction

The present essay originated in Professor C.G. Jung's seminar at the Eidgenossische Technische Hochschule (ETH), being the outcome of a report on a book which contained the visions of St. Perpetua. These visions made such an impression on me that I attempted their psychological interpretation.

One might well question both the sense of applying a modern form of psychological interpretation to this series of visions and the extent to which it is justifiable from the historical point of view. For such a method cannot fail to reveal connections which lie neither within Perpetua's own spiritual range nor within that of her time.

Perpetua actually interpreted her own visions, as the text shows. For instance, to her, the dragon of the first vision was the devil, whose aim it was to deter her from going the way of her martyrdom, while the shepherd who gave her the sweet-tasting food represented Christ. Her interpretations were accepted by the nascent Church of her day, and also later. Even today, their message remains compatible with Church teachings and meaningful for many.

Nevertheless, it seems to me that an attempt at an interpretation based on the scientific hypotheses of C.G. Jung's school of analytical psychology might throw light on some new and perhaps important factors.

The divine hypostases in the Christian conception of the world are accepted as absolute metaphysical reality in the dogma. They did not reveal themselves in some place outside the human sphere (which would be a contradiction in itself, inasmuch as revelation implies the human being who receives the message); thus we must conclude that these realities were experienced as a living totality—that is, by the human *soul* (the psyche). In fact, it was only in this way that such realities were able to become the formulated content of a creed—thanks to the testimony of human beings. It was the record in the Gospels and the witness of St. Paul that built up the image of Christ as we know it.

At the same time, it was above all the experiences of single individuals in visions and dreams (like those of St. Perpetua) which confirmed the collective faith—that is to say, the conviction that God had really become man in Christ. These individual experiences gave real foundation to the doctrine.

Dreams and visions are statements made by the human soul in a realm where consciousness and its conceptions are excluded. If we consider these spontaneous unconscious statements of the soul, we are able to perceive the Christian conception of the world originating in them as a phenomenon in itself. We can leave aside all that a philosophical knowledge, derived from the already existing cultures of antiquity, contributed to it, as well as all that was added by the theological interpretations and the theoretical and political deliberations of the ecclesiastical councils.

It is true that these additions were creative acts of human consciousness which gave meaning and reality to the soul's spontaneous statements, but at the same time these additions caught and imprisoned the statements of the soul in a formulation which was dependent on the historical situation, and consequently transitory. Therefore we are justified, I think, in attempting a new and wider formulation of the same phenomena from a modern psychological standpoint, though we are fully aware that this new interpretation must also be transitory.

Viewed from this perspective, it would be inadmissible to look upon the dragon of Perpetua's first vision simply and solely as the dogmatic figure of the devil. According to our scientific working hypothesis, we must take the dragon simply as it appears: that is to say, as a dream-image of a dragon, and inasmuch as it occurs frequently in myths and dreams, as the archetype of the dragon.

In this case the interpretation has to be reached through amplification, that is, by recalling similar images of dragons for comparison, a method which may not allow us to define the psychic meaning of the image by means of an abstract concept, but will enable us to describe it in a way which at least throws light upon the underlying energic processes.

For instance, the a priori interpretation of the dragon as the devil excludes every positive element in this figure, while the psychological way of considering it reveals quite unmistakably a positive as well as a negative aspect—a duality in the image of the dragon which throws a completely new light on the whole vision.

Naturally, the same argument applies to all the images and motifs appearing in the visions. As most of these are archetypal—which means that there exists a practically inexhaustible store of comparative material—I have confined myself principally to material from Perpetua's time, and have endeavored to show how these images appeared to people of that era in their conscious minds, and even more in spontaneous manifestations of the unconscious which welled up quite regardless of the consciously held creed.

This may perhaps lead to a new understanding of that significant epoch, inasmuch as the unprejudiced eye will then be able to perceive the birth of the Christian faith at its very source: in the soul of the human being at that time.

Figure 1. Saints Perpetua and Felicitas.
(From www.catholic-forum.com)

# 2
# The Text

The text of the "Passio Perpetuae et Felicitas," which describes the last days of the African martyrs Perpetua and Felicitas and their fellow sufferers, was discovered about the middle of the seventeenth century by Lukas Holsten among manuscripts coming from Monte Cassino. It was edited by P. Poussines and soon afterward—in the year 1668—was included in the *Acta Sanctorum*. A Greek version was found in Jerusalem in 1889 and published the following year.

Opinion is still divided as to which is the original text, but most scholars are inclined to look upon the Greek version either as an independent text or as a translation.[1]

A great number of noted theologians attribute the account to the Father of the Church, Tertullian. (The visions, on the other hand, are recorded by the martyrs themselves.) The proofs given by J.A. Robinson in his stylistic examination of the text are to my mind convincing evidence in favor of Tertullian's authorship.

Actually, Tertullian's claim is disputed mainly because, when making mention of the visions in his later writings, he says that Perpetua met only martyrs in the next world. This led to the conclusion that he had confused her visions with the vision of Saturus (a fellow martyr whose mandala vision is also recorded in the "Passio Perpetuae").[2] In my opinion, however, this refers—as Robinson points out—to the

---

[1] For the history of the text, see, among others "The Passion of St. Perpetua," in J.A. Robinson, *Texts and Studies: Contributions to Biblical and Patristic Literature,* vol. 1; and P. Franchi de Cavalieri, *La Passio SS. Perpetuae et Felicitatis.*

[2] See Tertullian, *de Anima* 55, 4. [For English, see A. Roberts and J. Donaldson, eds., *The Ante-Nicene Fathers: Translations of the Writings of the Fathers Down to A.D. 325,* vol. 5. Saturus's vision is given here in an appendix.—Ed.]

many people clad in white whom Perpetua, in her first vision, meets in the World Beyond.

In any case, Tertullian was in close connection with the martyrs whose sufferings are described in the text. Perpetua, Felicitas and their fellow martyrs (Saturninus, Secundulus, Renovatus and Saturus) were all put to death in Carthage in 203 A.D., during the time that Tertullian was its bishop.

# 3

# The Problem of the Orthodoxy
# of the Martyrs

Theologians have always differed on whether or not the martyrs belonged to the sect of the Montanists, which Tertullian himself joined about 205-207 A.D., a step which led to his break with the Church.[3]

Indeed, the author of the text appears to have had fairly strong Montanist leanings, but we do not know if the martyrs were of the same persuasion. The Montanist movement, which was by no means unimportant in Africa at that time, goes back to Lucius Montanus, a Phrygian from Pepuza who had presumably been a priest of Cybele before his conversion to Christianity.[4] We hear of him first about the middle of the second century. In fits of frenzied ecstasy accompanied by ravings and convulsions (as was customary in the Great Mother cults of Asia Minor), he poured forth new revelations in the name of the Paraclete or even in the names of God the Father and God the Son. He proclaimed himself to be the founder of a new "Church of the Spirit."

Among his female followers, Maximilla and Prisca were particularly conspicuous, chiefly for spreading prophecies concerning the coming end of the world. In fact the whole attitude of Montanism was closely bound up with this expectation. The movement was called "New Prophecy" and claimed that its oracles (imparted by the Spirit) marked a new era of revelation comparable to those of the Old and New Testaments.

---

[3] [For a psychological perspective on Tertullian and his association with the Montanists, see Edward F. Edinger, *The Psyche in Antiquity, Book 2: Gnosticism and Early Christianity,* pp. 105ff.—Ed.]

[4] See P. de Labriolle, *La Crise Montaniste.*

The Montanists divided history into three periods corresponding to the three hypostases of the Trinity—that of the Father, that of the Son and that of the Holy Ghost. Tertullian, for instance, says:

> So too, righteousness—for the God of righteousness and of creation is the same—was first in a rudimentary state, having a natural fear of God; from that stage it advanced, through the Law and the Prophets, to infancy; from that stage it passed, through the Gospel, to the fervor of youth; now, through the Paraclete, it is settling into maturity.

Thus the new revelation takes place through the Paraclete, whose coming after his death Christ had promised:

> And I will pray the Father, and he shall give you another Comforter [Paraclitum], that he may abide with you for ever; even the Spirit of Truth; whom the world cannot receive, because it seeth him not, neither know him: but ye know him; for he dwelleth with you, and shall be in you. (John 14: 16-17)[5]

The author of the "Passio Perpetuae" also emphasizes the approaching end, inasmuch as he refers to the Acts of the Apostles:

> And it shall come to pass in the last days, saith God, I will pour out of my Spirit upon all flesh: and your sons and daughters shall prophesy, and your young men shall see visions, and your old men shall dream dreams. (Acts 2:17)

He further admits that he recognizes later visions besides the prophecies of the Old and New Testaments as sources of revelation, by which he proves himself to be a Montanist. In view of the approaching second coming of Christ, the Montanists urged the observance of unusually severe penitential exercises and rigorously strict habits, and in this also Tertullian supported them. They called themselves *Pneumatikoi,* in contrast to the Catholic *Psychikoi,* and claimed, in opposition to the Catholic bishops, that they constituted

---

[5] [Biblical references throughout are to the Authorized King James Version.—Ed.]

the true spiritual Church of which only those who accepted the Paraclete could be members.

There were already Montanists in Rome about the year 200 A.D. (Their principal representatives were Proclus and Aeschines.) Judging by the papal decrees issued against the Montanists, the sect must have survived well into the eighth century. In spite of the movement's dogmatic orthodoxy, the Church opposed it on account of its wildly ecstatic and all too rigorous elements, its complete denial of the world, and the consequent danger that, on the ground of individual revelations, it might destroy the unity and temporal order of the Church—but above all because it recognized the right of women to teach. There is obviously a connection here with the orgiastic Great Mother cults of Asia Minor, and it would seem that the spirit of the latter must unconsciously have found its way into Montanism.

The Church itself, it is true, has never denied the possibility of divine revelation through dreams and visions, but these acquired far greater importance with the Montanists for they regarded them as the most evident manifestation of the Paraclete. In their religious ardor, and true to the spiritual attitude which led them to shun the world, they often sought a martyr's death of their own accord. We are inclined, therefore, to assume that the martyrs whose ecstatic behavior is particularly striking must have belonged to the Montanists, but it is just as probable that they had only been influenced by them, and had not yet gone far enough in this direction to be in conflict with the Church.

The psychological importance of the visions recorded in the "Passio Perpetuae," which is our chief concern, lies above all in the fact that they enable us to gain a deep insight into the unconscious spiritual situation of the time. We find archetypal images constellated in them which we also encounter in the literature of that epoch, when the *Weltanschauung* of antiquity was dissolving and the Christian conception of the world was breaking through. They appear here spontaneously in an unusual person, at an unusually tragic moment of her life, and lay bare the whole deep conflict of that time.

This record of an ancient series of four visions or dreams, occurring within a relatively short space of time (about fourteen days), is also quite exceptional. Usually the dreams handed down to us from antiquity—for instance by Artemidorus and Synesius—contain only single examples, and if there is any account of the conscious situation of the dreamer it is always insufficient.

# 4

# The Life of St. Perpetua

Where St. Perpetua is concerned, fortunately we are in possession of some facts. She came of a wealthy family, the Vibii, and at the time of her execution was twenty-two years of age. Her parents were still living, and her father—who was not a Christian—fought desperately up to the very last in hopes of prevailing upon his daughter to give up her resolve and recant.

Perpetua married quite young and had a son, whom she was still nursing and who was brought to her several times in prison. Strangely enough, her husband is never mentioned. She had two brothers, one of whom was likewise a catechumen.[6] A third brother, Dinocrates, who features in her second and third visions, had died a pagan at the age of seven.

Perpetua herself was baptized only twenty days before her death. She is reported to have said at the time:

> I was inspired by the Spirit not to ask for any other favor after the [baptismal] water but simply the perseverance [suffering] of the flesh.[7]

---

[6] [One who is being taught the principles of Christianity.—Ed.]

[7] Herbert Musurillo, trans., "Perpetua," in *The Acts of the Christian Martyrs*, p. 109.

# 5
# The Visions of St. Perpetua

Whereas the facts of her life and the description of her martyrdom are contributed by another hand, the visions—or rather dreams—are recorded by Perpetua herself. She had the first vision in prison after a visit from her brother. The text runs as follows:[8]

> My brother then said to me: "Sister, thou hast already traveled so far on the Christian road that thou canst now ask for a vision, and it shall be shown thee whether the passion awaits thee, or thy release."[9] And, mindful that I was in the habit of holding converse [colloquies] with God, who had so abundantly blessed me with his favors, and strong in faith and trust, I promised to report it to him [my brother] on the morrow. And I called [for the vision] and the following was shown to me:
>
> I beheld[10] a ladder of brass, of miraculous size, which reached up to Heaven, and was so narrow that it could only be ascended *singly*. On either side of the ladder, all manner of iron implements were fastened—swords, lances, hooks, daggers and spears—so that anyone who was careless, or who did not hold himself erect while climbing, was torn to pieces and remained hanging. Beneath the ladder was a gigantic dragon, lying in wait for the climbers and frightening them away.
>
> Saturus, however, went up before me (just as he later chose to be put to death first, for love of us, because he it was who had taught us, but afterward was not with us when we were thrown into prison). And he

---

[8] I have rendered the text of the visions myself from various sources, including W.H. Shewring, *The Passion of SS. Perpetua and Felicity;* E.C.E. Owen, *Some Authentic Acts of Early Martyrs;* and Roberts and Donaldson, eds., *The Ante-Nicene Fathers,* vol. 5, pp. 700ff.

[9] ["Passion" here refers to martyrdom, an archaic use of the word.—Ed.]

[10] Literally, "I behold." Perpetua uses the present tense of this verb both here and in the following visions.

reached the top of the ladder and, turning to me, spake: "Perpetua, I am holding thee, but see that the dragon does not bite thee." And I answered: "He shall not harm me, in the name of Jesus Christ." And the dragon slowly lifted his head out from under the ladder, as if in fear of me, and I trod on it, as though I were treading on the first rung of the ladder, and ascended to the top.

And I beheld a vast garden and, seated in the center of it, a tall white-haired man, in shepherd's dress, who was milking sheep, and round about him were many thousands of people clad in white. And he raised his head, looked at me, and spake: "It is well that thou art come, child!" And he called me to him and gave me also a morsel of the cheese which he was milking, and I received it with folded hands and ate. And all who stood round said, "Amen."

And at the sound of this invocation I awoke, and was aware that I was still eating something sweet, I know not what. And I immediately reported the vision to my brother, and we understood that it meant the coming passion. And from that time we began to put no more hope in this world.

The second vision, following her condemnation, goes like this:

A few days later, as we were all praying, a word suddenly burst from my lips, in the middle of the prayer, and I said, "Dinocrates!" And I started, for he had never entered my mind before, and I was pained at the recollection of his fate. And I knew immediately that I was held worthy to pray for him, and I began to intercede for him, and prayed at great length, lifting up my voice in lamentation.

And forthwith, in the same night, the following was shown to me: I beheld Dinocrates, coming forth from a dark place, where there were many other people, glowing with fever and thirsty, his face dirty and pale, and showing the wound in it which he had when he died. This Dinocrates had been my own brother, who succumbed to a cancer of the face at the age of seven in the most frightful circumstances, so that his death was a source of horror and dismay to everybody. It was for this child that I had prayed; and between myself and him there was a great distance, so that we could not reach one another.

In the place where Dinocrates stood there was also a *piscina* [basin], filled with water, whose rim was higher than the boy, and Dinocrates reached up as if to drink. But I was pained at the thought that the *piscina* was full of water, and yet that he could not drink on account of the height of its rim. And I awoke, and knew that my brother was in need, but I was confident that I would be able to help him in his need, and I prayed for him daily till we were taken over to the prison of the Proconsular palace; for we were to fight in the amphitheater. That was [just] the time of Caesar Geta's birthday. And I prayed for [Dinocrates], groaning and weeping night and day, that fulfillment might be granted me for his sake.

### Here is Perpetua's third vision:

The day that we remained in the prison I was shown the following: I beheld the same dark place which I had seen before (now quite light) and Dinocrates, with a clean body and well clothed, was refreshing himself.

And where the wound was, only a scar was to be seen; and the *piscina* which I had perceived before had lowered its rim to the height of the boy's navel, and he drank from it without ceasing, and on its edge stood a golden flask filled with water, and Dinocrates went up to it and began to drink out of it and it never became empty.

Content and happy, he then went off to play as children do—and I awoke. Then I understood that he had been removed from the place of punishment.

### The fourth vision follows:[11]

On the day before we were to fight [with the beasts], I saw the deacon Pomponius, in a vision, come to the prison door and knock violently. I went out and opened to him, and he wore a white festive toga, without a girdle, and manifold [elaborate] shoes, and he spake to me: "Perpetua, we are awaiting thee, come!"

And he took my hand, and we began to walk through a rough and pathless country. Toiling and panting, we came at length to the amphitheater

---

[11] In this account, I have followed the translation in Shewring, *The Passion of SS. Perpetua and Felicity.*

and he led me into the middle of the arena and spake to me: "Fear not, I am here with thee and shall fight with thee," and departed.

I beheld a huge crowd tense with expectation. And as I knew that I was to be brought before the beasts, I marveled that they were not let in. [Instead] an Egyptian of horrible appearance came out with his attendants to fight against me. Fair young men, my attendants and friends, came to me also and I was undressed and changed into a man.

My attendants began to rub me with oil, as was the custom before an *agon;* whereas I saw the Egyptian rolling himself in the dust. And there then came forth a man of miraculous size, so that he almost towered above the whole amphitheater, wearing a festive tunic, without a girdle, with a purple undergarment, which appeared across the middle of his chest between two other purple stripes falling from his shoulders and manifold shoes made of gold and silver.

He carried a rod, like a trainer of gladiators *[lanista],* and a green bough, on which hung golden apples. And he called for silence and spake: "This Egyptian here, if he is victorious, will kill her with the sword, and if she vanquishes him, she will receive this bough." Thereupon he withdrew.

And we fell upon each other and began to deal blows with our fists. He endeavored to seize me by the feet. But I trod upon his face with the soles of my feet and I was lifted up in the air and began to trample him as if I myself no longer touched the ground. But when I saw that I was getting no further in this way, I clasped my hands together and seized his head, then he fell upon his face and I trod upon his head. And the people began to shout and my assistants to jubilate.

I, however, went up to the *lanista* and received the bough. And he kissed me and spake: "Daughter, peace be with thee." Then, wreathed in glory, I began to go toward the gate of the pardoned *[porta sanavivaria].*

And I awoke and understood that it was not with the beasts, but against the devil that I should have to fight, but I knew the victory would be mine.

The main facts of the actual ensuing martyrdom, which were contributed by yet a third hand, are as follows.

When Perpetua was led into the arena, she and the others sang psalms in ecstatic exaltation. She was immediately knocked down by a mad cow which was let loose upon her, so that her dress tore, whereupon she tried anxiously to hide her nakedness and to put up her hair, which had fallen loose. Then she gave her hand to her fellow martyr Felicitas in order to help her rise.

The crowd could not help being impressed by such a scene and pardoned her to the extent that she should be put to death by the sword. The gladiator, who was a novice, thrust the sword into her ribs with an unsteady hand and hit bone. Perpetua groaned aloud, and according to an eyewitness,

> took the trembling hand of the young gladiator and guided it to her throat.
> . . . It was as though so great a woman, feared as she was by the unclean
> spirit, could not be dispatched unless she herself were willing.[12]

---

[12] Musurillo, trans., "Perpetua," in *Acts of the Christian Martyrs,* p. 131.

# 6
# Interpretation of the First Vision

That is the account of the "Passio Perpetuae." Concerning the genuineness of the visions, which is occasionally, if rarely, a subject of controversy,[13] the general impression they give seems somehow to banish any thought of their being a literary fiction.

Moreover, considered from a psychological point of view, they contain not a single purely Christian motif; rather, they contain only archetypal images common to the pagan, Gnostic and Christian worlds of that time. Had the visions been invented for the sake of edification, the author would most certainly have made use of exclusively Christian motifs. As it is, Christian authors have not known what to make of, for instance, Perpetua's transformation into a man in the last vision.

One would hardly, moreover, invent such an incident as that of Dinocrates' name suddenly jumping into Perpetua's mind—her second vision—when she should have been attending to her prayers, to say nothing of her dream, or fourth vision, the following night.

In addition, a psychological interpretation reveals a connecting inner thread running through all four visions, a thread that is by no means evident in the outer motifs. It only comes to light through the interpretation and, therefore, could not possibly have been invented by a person of that time.

Perpetua had the first of the visions or dreams as an answer to a definite question that had arisen in her consciousness: was she destined to suffer martyrdom or not? It was by no means uncommon at that time to call for or invite visions in this way; indeed, it was a generally widespread custom in both the pagan and Christian worlds. In the so-

---

[13] See Joh. J. Zimmermann, *Disquisitiones Historicae et Theologicae, de Visionibus.*

called incubation oracles it was customary to call upon the Deity for dreams in answer to definite questions. This practice, moreover, was not limited to the sacred places, and thus numerous prescriptions for bringing about true dreams have been preserved in the magic papyri.[14] Perpetua was confident of receiving an answer because, as she said, she "often held converse [conversations] with God."

The vision granted to her on the following night clearly states her psychological situation: she stands before a narrow ladder at the foot of which lies a dragon. This ladder leads up to a heavenly Garden of Eden. At first glance, the picture immediately recalls Jacob's ladder, which "reached to heaven" (Gen. 28:12), but the conception itself appears originally to have been old Egyptian, figuring in the Egyptian mysteries as a stair with seven gates or seven steps, symbolizing the seven planetary spheres through which the soul had to ascend to God after death. A *klimax heptapylos*—expressing the idea of ascending out of the different metals belonging to the planets (lead, tin, iron, mercury, an alloy for Venus, silver, gold) by means of a stair with seven gates—was likewise associated with the Mithraic mysteries.[15] The *heptaporos bathmis* (stair of seven steps) of the Chaldean oracles or the eighty steps of punishment in the cult of Mithras, mentioned by the mythographer Nonnos, were similar conceptions.

A further parallel is to be found in the visions of the philosopher Zosimos; he likewise sees in a dream an altar in the shape of a shallow bowl to which fifteen steps lead up.[16] There he perceives the place of the *askese,* or punishment, where people are cooked in boiling water

---

[14] [The so-called magic papyri is a collection of magical spells, formulas, hymns and rituals from Greco-Roman Egypt, second century B.C. to fifth century A.D. See Hans Dieter Betz, ed., *The Greek Magical Papyri in Translation: Including the Demotic Spells.*—Ed.]

[15] See F. Cumont, *Textes et monuments figurés relatifs aux mystères de Mithra,* II: 27.

[16] See "The Visions of Zosimos," *Alchemical Studies,* CW 13, pars. 85ff. [CW refers throughout to *The Collected Works of C.G. Jung]*

Figure 2. *Jacob's Ladder*, by William Blake.

in order that they may become *pneumata* (spirit beings).

The stair or ladder therefore has the meaning of a process of spiritualization, a development in the form of steps, leading to a higher state of consciousness.[17] Thus, for instance (as Professor Jung has brought to our notice), an alchemist, Blasius Vigenerus, says that "through the symbols, or signs, or attributes of God," which originate in the visible world, we "should be lifted up, as on a Jacob's ladder or Homer's golden chain, to the knowledge of the spiritual and intelligible things."[18]

This ascending process of transformation was sometimes dangerous and a real torture, as may be seen in the Zosimos visions. In Perpetua's vision there are iron implements fastened to the ladder to tear the unwary climber to pieces. Added to this, the ladder can only be climbed singly and there is no turning back. This picture undoubtedly contains a suggestion of her coming martyrdom. For instance, a contemporary source describes how the martyrs built, as it were, a ladder leading up to the gates of Heaven out of the steps of their sufferings, the instruments of their torture. It is surely for this reason that Perpetua's dream represents martyrdom in the form of a ladder, in order to convey that, seen from the psychic level, it has the meaning of a *transitus* to a higher state of consciousness; thus, the dream enables her to perceive the inner meaning of the event, the realization of which prepares her to meet her imminent fate.

The fact that the ladder can only be climbed singly shows that this road to higher consciousness is an individual path which ultimately must be trodden alone. The necessity of looking ahead—and on no account glancing back—is surely founded on the knowledge that when once the possibility of attaining a higher state of consciousness has arisen, one cannot return to a condition of unconsciousness without imperiling the soul. Indeed, the undertaking is fraught with such diffi-

---

[17] See *Psychology and Alchemy,* CW 12, par. 80.

[18] "Tractatus de Igne et Sale," in *Theatrum Chemicum,* VI:31.

culties that a single backward glance (as in the cases of Lot's wife and of Orpheus) suffices for a weak nature to be again overpowered by the tremendous force of the unconscious.

The idea that climbing upward on the ladder means a progression to a higher state of consciousness—and at the same time a painful *transitus*—is also expressed by the Syrian poet Jacob of Batnae, in regard to Sarug's singular conception of Jacob's ladder as a prefiguration of Christ's death upon the cross:

> The cross is set up as a wonderful ladder upon which mankind is in truth led up to heaven . . . . Christ arose upon earth as a ladder of many steps, and raised Himself on high, so that all earthly beings might be exalted through Him . . . . In the ladder, Jacob truly perceived the crucified one. . . . On the mountain, He [the Lord] made fast the mysterious cross, like a ladder, set Himself on the top of it and from thence blessed all the nations. . . . At that time, the cross was set up as a guiding ideal, as it were a ladder, and served all peoples as a path leading up to God.[19]

Saturus, later Perpetua's fellow martyr, now ascends before her (in the dream) and endeavors to instill courage into her. In reality this Saturus had not been imprisoned at the same time as Perpetua, Felicitas and their other fellow martyrs, but he subsequently behaved toward the authorities in such an aggressive way that he likewise ended up in prison. He did this deliberately in order to be able to help the others spiritually and strengthen them in their faith. So he was one of those who sought a martyr's death passionately and of their own free will. That is the reason why Perpetua interprets her dream—in this respect—objectively, as an anticipation of the real event, just as the instruments of torture attached to the ladder led her to conclude that she would have to face martyrdom.

---

[19] My translation, from "Die Vision Jakobs von Beth-El," in P.S. Landesdörfer, ed., *Ausgewählte Schriften der syrischen Dichter*, p. 87. As Professor Jung brought to my notice, the Virgin Mary was also described as *scala efferens a terra in coelum.* (Pitra, *Analecta sacra*, I, p. 264)

Undoubtedly the whole vision has a "prognostic" value, but when we compare the entire proceeding in it with the actual fulfillment, it becomes evident that it has been transferred to the mythological level. For instance, martyrdom is not represented as such but as a ladder leading up to heaven; and it is a dragon—in other words a purely mythological figure—that tries to hinder Perpetua's ascent. It is as though the dream were intent on representing the real and deeper meaning of the event threatening the dreamer in the outer world in order thereby to prepare her for her inescapable fate. Therefore it displays the archetypal background of this fate.

In such an inner connection, Saturus also becomes a symbolic image: he represents the Christian spiritual attitude of the fanatical believer, or in other words a Christian animus figure in Perpetua herself.

As the unconscious consists in the first place of all the parts of the personality which—mainly for reasons of outer adaptation—have not been integrated into consciousness, its character is specifically complementary to that of consciousness. It is therefore usually embodied in an archetypal figure of the opposite sex which transmits the contents of the collective unconscious. Hence, by "animus," we mean the personification of all the masculine components of a feminine personality, a woman's unlived traits which have remained in the unconscious background.

In the case of a man, the anima embodies chiefly his affects, feelings and emotions, while a woman's animus represents rather an a priori opinion or conviction of a collective nature which arises from the unconscious. A conviction of this kind can indeed take possession of a woman with such demonic and passionate force that it is capable of completely destroying her feminine existence. But the animus also possesses creative power: it is the *logos spermatikos* (the spermatic Word) which transmits new contents from the unconscious.[20]

---

[20] See "Anima and Animus," *Two Essays on Analytical Psychology,* CW 7, par. 336; also Emma Jung, "On the Nature of the Animus," in her *Animus and Anima.*

Inasmuch as Perpetua—judging from the slender knowledge we possess of her personal life—had lived a thoroughly feminine existence as a wife and mother, all her traditionally masculine traits such as courage, determination, the power to stand unflinchingly by a conviction even in the face of death—traits which break through to a striking extent in her martyrdom—are chiefly embodied in the unconscious animus figure and are projected onto Saturus who, we are told, first converted her to Christianity.

*[margin note: unconscious power of archetypes]*

In other words, she experiences and sees in Saturus these qualities which he evidently actually possessed to a high degree. Hence it becomes apparent through the dream that Perpetua's Christian spiritual attitude was not mainly a consciously integrated one, acquired through the Christian teaching (which was indeed unlikely, seeing that the latter had been of such very short duration). It was rather a passionate conviction which arose from the unconscious, a spiritual state of emotional possession which took hold of her completely and drew her fatefully into the collective problem of her time—the problem to which her individual existence was destined to succumb.

When the dream depicts Saturus ascending the ladder before her, it shows precisely—on the subjective level—that this masculine spiritual attitude in Perpetua herself, which had hitherto remained unconscious, has now taken over the lead. The unconscious thus parallels consciousness and supports it in the fulfillment of a new type, that of the Christian.

At the foot of the ladder, however, lies a dragon which endeavors to prevent her from climbing. In Christian imagery the dragon, or serpent, has become a symbol for the devil, as "leviathan . . . the dragon that is in the sea" (Isa. 27:1), or as the tempter in the Garden of Eden. In most dualistic religious systems the dragon generally plays the role of a chthonic, wicked demon, the enemy of light, usually of a feminine nature. As a cold-blooded animal, however, with a very small development of the cerebrum, the serpent chiefly signifies the system of reflexes (the basal ganglia and the spinal cord), the instinctive psyche or "nature-spirit," or simply the unconscious. As far back as the teaching of the Gnostic sect of the Perates, the serpent was identified with the cerebellum and the spinal cord. In the macrocosm the Father corresponded to the cerebrum, but the cerebellum was associated with the Son, the Redeemer—that is, with the serpent (as Logos). The serpent conveyed the pneumatic substance to the spinal cord which in turn brought forth the seed of all creatures.[21]

In pre-Christian antiquity, in Gnosticism and also in its medieval continuation, alchemy, the serpent signifies not only an ambiguous and concealed Deity but also a sacred demon dispensing blessings—a true Redeemer. Thus the Perates also say that the all-encompassing serpent (that is, the Ouroboros, tail-eating dragon, Figure 3) which as Oceanus surrounds the earth like a ring, is the wise Logos of Eve, the *mysterium* of Eden, the river that flows out of Eden (Eden is the brain) and divides into the four origins. And as "the serpent of brass" which Moses "put upon a pole" (Num. 21:9), it becomes a symbol of Christ, the *Soter*-serpent. In Egypt also the dragon was principally worshipped as a serpent of salvation, as the outward form of the god of revelation, Hermes, as the *Agathodaimon* (Figure 4, page 34), or as Osiris, "lord of the Egyptian earth" and husband of Isis.

In the Roman catacombs, in the so-called Balbina *coemeterium*,[22] there is a remarkable fresco which is looked upon as an illustration of Perpetua's vision: a human figure is ascending a ladder under which lies a serpent. The ladder rises out of a corn field consisting of single tall ears of corn. So here the serpent represents the earth spirit connected with the corn fields. This points even more clearly to the Egyptian *Agathodaimon* that was worshipped as "cornfield head" and *Pantokrator*.

---

[21] Hippolytus, *Elenchos* V, 17, pp. 11ff.

[22] See Fernand Cabrol, ed., *Dictionnaire d'Archéologie Chrétienne et de Liturgie*, vol. 2, col. 151, and also under "Balbina."

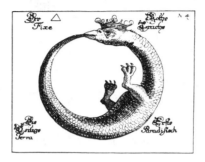

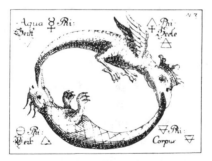

Figure 3. The Ouroborus as crowned dragon (top) and
winged and wingless serpents.[23]

---

[23] [From Eleazar, *Uraltes chymisches Werk* (1760), part 2, nos. 4 and 3 (Mellon Coll.,
Yale University Library).—Ed.]

Figure 4. *Agathodaimon* on Gnostic gem and amulet.[24]

The Gnostic Ophites also interpreted the ear of corn which was shown in the Eleusinian Mysteries as the Logos which rules the world. It is a symbol for all the dying and resurrecting vegetation gods such as Attis, Osiris, Adonis, the Phrygian Papas and so forth.

In this connection the dragon is clearly a symbol for an "unconscious nature-spirit," "the wisdom of the earth." Therefore, seen from the Christian standpoint, it also represents the pagan conception of the world in which experience of the Deity, or of the spirit, was projected into the material reality of the world. In antiquity, one experienced divinity through a feeling of being gripped and moved by the phenomena of nature—in the rustling of the Dodonean oaks, in the murmuring of a fountain, in the starry heavens and the glow of the rising sun. These were the manifestations of the highest power. This form of experience, however, had obviously become unsatisfying, even destructive, and it had to be surmounted rather than overcome.

The process of withdrawing the projection of the gods from nature had actually already begun in the Stoa. They interpreted the Olympians as the embodiment of specific psychic characteristics, but only

---

[24] [From Charles William King, *The Gnostics and Their Remains: Ancient and Medieval*, plate 3, figs. 7 and 2.—Ed.]

again in favor of a "subtle material" conception of the spirit, as having a fiery, ethereal nature—the all-pervading and all-ruling *Nous.* But it was Christianity which first took the real step toward a purely spiritual, extramundane conception of God. It is the realization of this fact which is represented in Perpetua's ascent over and beyond the dragon to a heavenly place. Consequently in the vision, the dragon stands for the danger of slipping back into the old pagan spiritual attitude, out of which the ladder shows the way to higher consciousness.

As a feminine and chthonic being, however, the dragon also means Perpetua's own instinctive soul, her will to live and her feminine reality which she tramples underfoot and disregards as she steps beyond.

In the *Shepherd of Hermas,* we also find—as J.A. Robinson has pointed out—the image of a gigantic animal symbolizing the anti-Christian power. It is a beast resembling a sea monster, about a hundred feet in length with a head like an earthenware vessel. This recalls the demonic angel Amnaël in the old alchemical text, *Isis to Horus.* On his head, as a *semeion* (sign or symbol), he carries just such a vessel, containing the alchemical secret substance Isis is seeking.[25]

The motif of the vessel as the head itself, or even as *on* the head, points to a feminine *mysterium,* so these parallels confirm what is already clear to us—namely, that Perpetua rejects her own feminine instinct in order to attain spiritual transformation. In so doing she treads on the dragon's head. This is a well-known gesture of triumph and, as St. Augustine (who often refers to the "Passio Perpetua," and appears to have been very much impressed by it) already recognized,[26] probably is also an allusion to Genesis 3:15:

> And I will put enmity between thee and the woman, and between thy seed and her seed; it shall bruise thy head, and thou shalt bruise his heel.

---

[25] See M. Berthelot, *Collection des Anciens Alchemistes Grecs.*
[26] Germ. 280. See Jacques Paul Migne, ed., *Patrologiae cursus completus,* Latin series, vol. 38, col. 1282.

The trampling of the dragon, according to Psalms 91:13—"the young lion and the dragon shalt thou trample under feet" *(et concul-cabis leonem et draconem)*—was also frequently looked upon at that time as a sign of martyrdom and as victory over the devil.

On reaching the top of the ladder, Perpetua finds herself in a garden, in the center of which a gigantic shepherd, clad in white, is milking sheep. As this garden lies in Heaven above, it can be no other than the celestial garden, Paradise, the Heavenly World Beyond; and this is also the reason why, immediately on waking, Perpetua interprets the dream as a premonition of her approaching death. It is in the garden that she is received into the bright company of the Blessed, robed in white.

The idea that Paradise should again become the abode of humanity after death is already foreshadowed in the Apocryphal Books of the Old Testament. Perpetua's vision, and especially Saturus's vision of Paradise, included further on in the "Passio Perpetuae," in which he enters into a heavenly garden with cypresses and roses, facing the east, are among the earliest known Christian conceptions of Paradise.

Curiously enough, the idea of Paradise led to a long dogmatic discussion. According to prevailing opinion at the time, it is a *locus corporalis,* a material place occupying a definite space where the souls abide, in contrast to the extramundane Heavenly kingdom, the "Father's Mansion," for which it is a preliminary stage. According to the Church Father Hippolytus, it exists on earth toward the east.[27]

Another conception, however, places Paradise beyond the cosmos. In the *Passio SS. Montani et Lucii,* for example, Christ appears—in the figure of a boy with a shining countenance—to a fellow martyr named Victor, and promises him eternal life. When the latter asks where Paradise is to be found, Christ answers: *"Extra mundum"* (beyond the world). Indeed, Origen had to refute a conception according

---

[27] Hippolytus, *Hexaemeron,* in Migne, ed., *Patrologiae,* Greek series, vol. 10, col. 585.

to which Paradise "is only an immaterial world, existing merely in the fantasies of the mind and in thought."[28] Philo was already familiar with this interpretation and himself held that Paradise is a symbol of God's wisdom.

The localization of Paradise outside the cosmos is explained by the idea that its four rivers, with their purifying and fertilizing properties, had their origin in the division of "the waters which were under the firmament from the waters which were above the firmament" (Gen. 1:7). These celestial waters very early on in the patristic literature became a symbol for the Holy Ghost. From this primordial place the power of God created the four rivers of Paradise, so that the latter were somehow regarded as identical with them.[29]

Since Perpetua does not journey over the face of the earth toward the east, but rather climbs up a ladder to Heaven, the Paradise of her vision must be the extramundane Paradise. In psychological language, the higher level of consciousness which she seeks to attain is thus revealed as a spiritual reality beyond the material world and the cosmos. In this reality, ideas exist in themselves and are no longer experienced as projected into the universe.

The curious uncertainty concerning the material position of Paradise in space no doubt comes from the fact that Christianity did not recognize that its own conception of God and its most important dogmas primarily reside within the soul as psychological realities (which indeed was quite impossible to realize at the time, as is proved by Origen's refutation mentioned above). Instead, they were projected as absolutes in a space beyond the world—with the result that these ideas again acquired a peculiar substantiality.

---

[28] Origen, *de Principiis*, 1, II, chap. 3. For English, see Roberts and Donaldson, eds., *Ante-Nicene Fathers*.

[29] [For further elaboration of the psychological significance of the four rivers, see Edward F. Edinger, *The Aion Lectures: Exploring the Self in C.G. Jung's* Aion, pp. 139ff.—Ed.]

In Perpetua's vision, in the middle of the garden the "Good Shepherd" receives the Saint and gives her "a morsel of the cheese which he was milking." The figure of the shepherd as a guiding spirit, a *Paredros* and Redeemer, was an archetypal concept common to the pagan and Christian worlds of that time.[30] In the pagan world, he was called the Poimandres (Figure 5), "shepherd of men" (an aspect of Hermes), who leads them to enlightenment and redeems them. He became the prototype for the shepherd in the Christian text, the *Shepherd of Hermas*, which Robinson—quite rightly, it seems to me—looks upon as the source of the text under discussion.

The text entitled *Poimandres* begins with the following description of the ecstatic vision of a Hermetist:

> Methought there came to me a Being of overwhelming and boundless proportions, who called me by name and spake: "What do you wish to hear and see and know by thought?"
>
> "Who are you?" I said.
>
> "I," said he, "am the Poimandres, the Spirit of Truth *[ho tes authentias nous]*.[31] I know what you wish, for indeed *I am with you everywhere.*"
>
> "I would fain learn," I said, "the things that are, and understand their nature and acquire knowledge of God." He answered me: "Keep in mind all you desire to learn, and I will teach you!" When he had thus spoken, he changed his semblance, and forthwith all things were opened out in a moment, as by a sudden turn of the scale [rope], and I beheld a boundless vision, I saw all creation as a most mild and joyous light.[32]

It is not only in the Hermetic writings that this God of Redemption and leader of souls appears as a symbol of *Nous,* or Logos, in the form

---

[30] See R. Reitzenstein, *Poimandres.*

[31] Scott endeavors to prove that *authentia* means sovereignty, omnipotence, but from my point of view the meaning of genuineness or truth is nearer the sense in this case. Perhaps the nearest rendering would be Spirit of Absoluteness.

[32] My own rendering of the Greek text in *Corpus Hermeticum,* book 1, in W. Scott, ed., *Hermetica.*

Figure 5. The Poimandres, shepherd of men.
(Museum of the Acropolis, Athens)

of a shepherd. Attis, who is interpreted as *Anthropos* and Logos in the Sermon of the Naassene, is a "shepherd of the shining stars." In like manner the Phrygian Zeus or Papas was pictured by the Gnostics as a goatherd. They interpreted the Greek word *Aipolos* (goatherd) as *Aeipolos* (the ever-rotating one); that is, the all-transforming and generating Logos.

The same applies to the Egyptian God Anubis, and to the Egyptian sun-god, Horus. In the *Egyptian Book of the Dead,* the latter is the "good shepherd" who rules over the "four human races," which form his flock.

The shepherd is a cosmic figure and, at the same time, is generally also considered the first man, the *Anthropos*.[33] As a text says, he is "the son of God, who can do everything and become everything as he will [and] appears to any one as he will." He extends throughout the universe and is the redeemer from the compulsion of the stars, the *heimarmene.*

But why should just the image of the shepherd have been chosen for this conception of God and as a symbol of *Nous?* Philo of Alexandria endeavors to explain it as follows:

> The role of shepherd is such an exceedingly good one, that it is not only ascribed to kings and wise men, and to the souls which have been purified through initiation, but also, and rightly, to God himself, the leader of the universe. For, as if in a meadow or pasture, the Shepherd and King-God, with justice and law, leads his great flock: the earth and the water, the air and the fire, and all that in them is, plants and living beings, mortal and immortal, and also the nature of the heavens, and the circlings of sun and moon, and the rhythmic dances of the stars. He sets over them his upright Word [Logos], his first-born Son, who will receive the charge of this holy flock as the vice-regent of the Great King.[34]

---

[33] Therefore in Perpetua's vision, as in the *Poimandres,* he is of supernatural stature.

[34] Philo, *de Agricultura,* 50. My rendering of the Greek text. [For English, see F.H. Colson and G.H. Whitaker, *Philo with an English Translation.*—Ed.]

Thus the shepherd was a symbol of the ordering mind of God, the Stoic *Nous* or Logos, which pervades the whole universe. Therefore he carries the staff of king and judge, with which he rules. He is a *"pneuma* reaching from heaven to earth."

At that time, humanity looked upon the laws of nature chiefly as the effects of a in-dwelling semi-material and divine spirit. But this spirit had now "become man"; it was no longer merely the power of nature but also a *daimon paredros,* personally experienced by each individual. Numerous prayers in the pagan *Magic Papyri* are addressed to this spirit which pervaded and ruled the cosmos; for instance:

> Hail, thou who comest forth from the four winds, Pantokrator, thou who breathest the life-giving *pneuma* into man . . . whose eyes are the sun and moon, shining in the pupils of man . . . thou are the Agathodaimon, who generates everything and nourishes the inhabited earth.[35]

Or again:

> Thou who sittest on the head of the cosmos, and judgest everything, surrounded by the circle of truth and faith. Thou who bearest on thy head the golden crown, and in thy hand the staff with which thou sendest forth the gods.[36]

He was usually represented as a beggar with staff and knapsack, as the power that holds the cosmos together and as the "shepherd of the stars," that is, the center of all the innumerable celestial constellations. From the psychological point of view, this primordial image of the shepherd represents the Self, whence all the other archetypal images of the collective unconscious receive their invisible regulation.

Christ as the Good Shepherd and *Pantokrator* has taken over all the functions of the pagan god. He is a liberator from the *heimarmene;* as *Kosmokrator* he likewise extends throughout the universe. He is called

---

[35] Karl L. Preisendanz, ed., *Papyri Magicae Graecae,* vol. 1, p. 107.
[36] Ibid.

the all-powerful Logos of God, "who walking on earth, touches the heavens." In contemporary art he often figures as a kind of Hermes, a lamb on his shoulders, over his head the seven planets, on either side of him sun and moon, and at his feet seven lambs, representing the seven nations. On an epitaph in the Domitilla *coemeterium,* he is even depicted as Attis with a shepherd's staff and pipe. The *Martyrium Polycarpi* (chap. 19) calls him "the shepherd of the Universal Church which extends all over the world," and in the Alberkios inscription he is "the holy shepherd, who feeds his flocks of sheep on mountains and plains."

In a saying such as the opening verses of Psalm 23—"The Lord is my shepherd; I shall not want"—which St. John in the New Testament applies to Christ (John 10:11-16), he is still quite definitely thought of as a kind of *daimon paredros*—that is, as a personal guardian spirit that accompanies each individual, just in the same way as the Poimandres declares, "I am with you everywhere." In the *Martyrium Polycarpi* (chap. 19), he is even called "the shepherd, the savior of our souls and *the guide of our bodies.* "

Thus he is, so to speak, a nonpersonal guiding spirit, yet also in some way connected with the ego, almost in the sense of an apparition, which means that at that time the unconscious no longer appeared as a power projected into nature, but rather as a daimon accompanying man. This is shown most impressively in the appearance of the shepherd described by Hermas:

> While I was praying at home, seated on my bed, there entered a man of lordly appearance, *in shepherd's garb,* clad in a white goat skin, his pack on his shoulders and a staff in his hand; and he greeted me, and I returned the greeting.
>
> Forthwith he sat down by me, saying: "I am sent by the highest angel, that I may dwell with thee all the remaining days of thy life."
>
> I suspected that he had come to tempt me, and asked: "Who art thou? For I know into whose keeping I was given."
>
> He said to me: "Dost thou not know me?"

"No," I replied.

Then he declared: "I am the shepherd into whose care thou hast been given." And while he was still speaking he changed his semblance, and I knew that he was the one into whose keeping I had been given.[37]

The shepherd then undertakes the function of strengthening Hermas in his faith and instructing him.

As we shall see, something of the same kind takes place in Perpetua's vision when, in a scene which recalls the Holy Communion, the shepherd gives her a morsel of cheese and she receives it with folded hands. This scene in particular has been looked upon as a proof that the martyrs were Montanists, for a special group among them, the so-called Artotyrites—from *artos* (bread) and *tyros* (cheese)—are said to have celebrated their Eucharist not with wine but with bread and cheese. In any case, the manner in which the cheese is dispensed in the vision is entirely modeled on the partaking of the Holy Communion.

Some writers have also seen a certain connection in this passage with the *Passio Montani*, which describes the passion of "a certain Montanus" and his followers. As a result of the death of the proconsul these martyrs were doomed to linger a considerable time in prison. Several of their visions which have been recorded are not unlike St. Perpetua's. For instance, a woman named Quartillosia had the vision of a young man of supernatural stature who fed the prisoners with two bowls of milk that never became empty and promised them a third, after which he disappeared through the window.

The singular picture in the St. Perpetua vision of the shepherd milking cheese (which moreover could occur only in a genuine dream) probably comes from the fact that two conceptions overlap: the idea of the Holy Communion, the receiving of the Host, as something "made by the hand of man," something solid; and, on the other hand,

---

[37] My rendering of the text in Reitzenstein, *Poimandres,* p. 11.

the idea of bestowing a drink in the form of milk.

In the Phrygian mysteries, for instance, the mystic abstained from eating meat "and moreover he fed on milk as one newly born." This is important inasmuch as Montanus himself was a Phrygian. Milk and honey were also looked upon as stimulating and inspiring, much the same as wine. In a magic papyrus we read: "Drink milk and honey before sunrise, and in thy heart there will be something divine." Milk also stood for spiritual teaching in the Christian world: "As newborn babes, desire the sincere milk of the word *[logikon]*, that ye may grow thereby: if so be ye have tasted that the Lord is gracious." (1 Pet. 2:2). And:

> Ye have need that one teach you again which be the first principles of the oracles of God; and are become such as have need of milk, and not of strong meat. For everyone that useth milk is unskilful in the word of righteousness: for he is a babe. (Heb. 5:12-13; also 1 Cor. 3:2)

St. Paul described himself and his followers as "children in Christ" *(nepioi en Christo),* and Clement of Alexandria even calls the Christians directly, *galaktophagoi* (milk-drinkers). Milk too stands for an emanation of the Deity. In the so-called *Odes of Solomon* we read:

> A cup of milk was offered to me; and I drank it in the sweetness of the delight of the Lord. The Son is the cup, and He who was milked is the Father: and the Holy Spirit milked him: because his breasts were full, and it did not seem good to Him that His milk should be spilt for nought; and the Holy Spirit opened her bosom and mingled the milk from the two breasts of the Father; and gave the mixture to the world [literally, "aeons"], without its knowing it; and they who receive [it] are in the perfection of the right hand [literally, "on the right hand in the *Pleroma"].*[38]

As Reitzenstein doubtless rightly interprets it, the drink of milk denotes the beginning, and the draught of wine, on the other hand, the

---

[38] J.H. Bernard, ed., *The Odes of Solomon,* in J.A. Robinson, *Texts and Studies,* vol. 8, no. 3, Ode 19.

complete fulfillment of man's divinity.[39] According to the rules of the Church instituted by Hippolytus, the neophytes first received a cup of water, then a mixture of milk and honey, and finally wine and water as the real Eucharist.

The sweet-tasting morsel which Perpetua receives at the hands of the shepherd is thus a kind of spiritual food, or teaching, through which she is admitted to the bright company of the Blessed (those who stand around robed in white and say "Amen"), the company in the Beyond, whence—in the fourth vision—comes the deacon Pomponius, in festive garb, to fetch her away. It also has the meaning of a *cibus immortalis,* an immortal food, inasmuch as those "who worship God in spirit and in truth have a share in his glory and are immortal with him in that they are partakers of eternal life through the Logos." The Holy Ghost was indeed a life-giving breath.

If the gods of antiquity were already dead—that is, if the highest value bestowing life and giving it meaning had sunk at that time into the unconscious and become dissolved—this value had risen again in a changed form in the figure and teaching of Christ, the God become man and mediator. The unconscious life force streamed forth from the new teaching, enabling life to progress on a fresh course and bringing about a step forward in culture.[40]

The first of Perpetua's visions describes this process in archetypal images. It is true that the complex meaning in their deeper connections could hardly have been accessible to her consciousness, but they did give her the inner feeling of a meaning in her destiny. Thus, they enabled her to accept her martyrdom.[41]

---

[39] *Hellenistische Mysterienreligionen,* p. 330.

[40] For the problem of the death of the god, see "Psychology and Religion," *Psychology and Religion,* CW 11, pars. 145ff.

[41] [This is after all in the nature of archetypal images which, as anyone who has undergone depth analysis can attest, impinge on consciousness at times of deep personal strife.—Ed.]

Although the dream represents the Christian teaching as the highest value and as a new source of life, one can hardly assume that the unconscious intended to drive Perpetua into martyrdom. The obstructing factor in itself, for instance, is by no means exclusively characterized as a power of evil, although Perpetua interprets it as the devil. The dragon may also represent the unconscious animal side which seeks to hinder Perpetua's ascent and which she tramples underfoot. Quite objectively, the dream simply lays before our eyes the inner process which is taking place.

The suprapersonal imagery is the language of the collective unconscious. The impressive power and depth of the images can no doubt be explained by the fact that they were called forth as a vital reaction of the unconscious to the fate threatening the dreamer in the outer world.

# 7

# Interpretation of the
# Second and Third Visions

Perpetua's second vision contains a piece of the more personal side of her problem in a language that is more accessible to her conscious world, although it touches upon the same basic motifs that appeared in the first vision.

This is the dream of the little brother, Dinocrates, in the underworld. The Roman Catholic Church takes such visions very concretely and uses them as a basis for its doctrine of the intercession of saints, which has the effect of succoring the souls in Purgatory. (Perpetua herself seems to have interpreted the dream in this sense.)

If, however, we consider the dream on the subjective level —that is, in the first place as an inner event—Dinocrates (like Saturus in the first vision) undoubtedly embodies a spiritual content in Perpetua herself. His suffering, as portrayed in the dream, is in some way identical with her own painful condition. This suffering should therefore be understood as the inner need that caused her to yearn for the "fountain of living water," the baptismal water.

To Perpetua, this little brother who died in early childhood, together with all the memories which are linked with him, represents a piece of her own past, something childlike, a spirit in herself as yet unbaptised for whom the redeeming truth, symbolized by the water, is literally "too high." This is shown by the fact that the edge of the *piscina* (pool) is beyond the child's reach. Between Perpetua and this little brother there is a "great distance,"[42] which means that consciously she is far removed from this childish spiritual attitude, though

---

[42] See Luke 16:26.

it still clings to her. And this is also corroborated by the fact that she tells us she had not thought of him for a long time.

This childish piece of paganism in Perpetua—the dream figure Dinocrates—is suffering from a cancer; that is to say, he is subjected to a state of inner decay which cannot be arrested. Thus the dream points to a regression, or rather to a difficulty which has arisen in Perpetua's inner development, which is perhaps the danger of allowing herself to be influenced by her father, who strove with all his might and all the authority he possessed to have her recant her faith. (This is probably why her resistance to the Christian attitude is represented as a "child in the family.") Apparently a more childish unconscious spirit is still alive in Perpetua, one threatened with decay, one for whom the Christian truth is out of reach so that she yearns in vain for its redeeming effect.

Franz Josef Dölger, in his essay on the Dinocrates vision, points out that this picture of the underworld coincides exactly with the pagan concept of Hades, rather than with the Christian notion of Purgatory. Thus, the pagan in Dinocrates is even more clearly emphasized.[43] It also recalls the description of the underworld in the *Book of Enoch* (chap. 22), as divided into a dark place for sinners and a light place, in the middle of which there is a "bright spring of water."

The idea that the dead suffer from thirst in the underworld is again an ancient and widespread idea that is also found in the third vision of the *Shepherd of Hermas*. Dölger goes on to prove that the vision here refers to the belief, prevalent in antiquity, that those who had died before their time or had suffered a violent death, underwent particular torment in Hades and could only be delivered through the prayers of the living.[44]

Looked at from a psychological point of view, this idea is the sym-

---

[43] See *Antike Parallelen zum leidenden Dinocrates ub der Passio Perpetuae, Antike und Christentum*, vol. 2, pp. 1ff.

[44] Ibid.

bolic representation of the fact that contents of the unconscious, which are split off and unable to live fully in reality, become negative and appear as ghosts seeking release, so to speak. In other words, they cause psychological disturbances, as seems to be the case here where just such a split-off content belonging to Perpetua's childhood is concerned.

When the pagan attitude in Perpetua is represented as a child, the dream may possibly be alluding to the fact that pagan consciousness is relatively infantile when compared to the Christian attitude. Rufinus, at all events, has expressed this view:

> He [a saint] taught all men that they should direct their minds away from the visible and material things to the invisible and immaterial. "It is indeed time," he said, "that we turned to an occupation of this kind, for we cannot always remain boys and children, but must now once for all rise to the higher spiritual things and become grown men."[45]

In the third vision, shortly before Perpetua's death, Dinocrates again appears to her, transfigured and redeemed by the water of life. The decaying wound on his face is healed over, and he "went off to play as children do." Thus, he had become the image of one reborn *in novam infantiam* and, as such, his fate also represents a forecast of Perpetua's own situation and development.[46] For, whereas in the second and third visions she experiences everything in the person of Dinocrates or as an onlooker, in the fourth dream she herself is confined in the dark prison and has to take up the fight with the spirit of darkness in order to receive the bough of the tree of life.

A modern dream should be mentioned here, one which contains the

---

[45] [The source for this passage could not be found, but the Rufinus referred to is probably Tyrannius Rufinus of Aquileia, a fourth-century associate but later antagonist of St. Jerome. See this Web site: www.ocf.org/OrthodoxPage/reading/St.Pachomius/Xrufin.html.—Ed.]

[46] Concerning the anticipatory character of the child archetype, see Karl Kerényi and C.G. Jung, *Essays on a Science of Mythology,* pp. 83f.

same symbolism in a most striking way, and which, moreover, arose
out of a situation similar to Perpetua's.[47] It is the dream of the Roman Catholic student Sophie Scholl, a girl of twenty-one who was
guillotined in Munich for spreading anti-Nazi propaganda. In prison
the night before her death, she dreamed that on a beautiful sunny day
she was carrying a child in a long white robe to its christening. The
way to the church led up a steep mountain but "firm and safe" she
carried the child in her arms. Suddenly, without warning, a crevasse
opened in front of her. She had only enough time to lay the child
safely down before she crashed into the depths.

In reality Sophie died with immense courage. She herself interpreted her dream in the sense that the child's white robe stood for the
idea for which her own death prepared the way. The steep path up to
the church recalls the ladder of Perpetua's first vision, which represented the difficult way of individuation. The fate of the child that
has not yet been christened points to Dinocrates. The abyss is an image of the "jaws of death" which swallow up the mortal side, whereas
the Divine Child—the Self in the process of becoming—lives on.

One can hardly help being deeply moved and impressed by the way
in which the unconscious reacts: without the faintest sentimentality
but with unerring certainty, it represents the real, significant inner
process and conveys symbolically the absolute knowledge which provides real support.

The pitiful condition of little Dinocrates in Hades and his redemption recall most vividly the contemporary alchemical concepts of
those "bound in Hades" who yearned for the divine water, the *hydor
theion.* In the *Treatise of Comarius to Cleopatra,* for instance, we read
that the holy waters descended from on high to visit the dead—
prostrate, chained and crushed in the darkness of Hades—and that the
*pharmakon zoes* (medicine of life) penetrated them and revived them;

---

[47] For this material I am indebted to Hildegard Nagel. [Miss Nagel was a regular par-
ticipant in Jung's early seminars.—Ed.]

and he (the spirit) clothed them in divine and spiritual glory, and they came out of the earth. And it was said:

They array themselves in light and glory; in that they had increased in accordance with nature, and their figures had been transformed, and they had arisen from sleep, and had come forth from Hades. The body of the fire had given them birth. [Compare Dinocrates' feverish heat *(aestus)!]* . . . and as they came forth from it they clothed themselves in glory, and it [the body of the fire] brought them complete oneness, and the image was fulfilled through body, soul and spirit, and they became one.[48]

Dinocrates drinks the water from a golden flask, which also strikes one as a remarkably alchemical motif. It recalls the vessel of Hermes *(vas Hermetis)* which was in some way imagined to be consubstantial with its contents. In the Hermetic treatise *The Krater,* we read that after God had created the universe, he filled a vessel, a kind of baptismal font (compare the *piscina),* with *Nous* and sent it down to earth, so that people who dipped themselves in it should receive a share of *ennoia* (consciousness, enlightenment).[49]

We find another Christian vision which parallels Perpetua's in the *Passio SS Mariani et Jacobi.* A martyr named Marianus found himself transported in a dream to a heavenly grove of pines and cypresses:

In the middle there stood the overflowing basin of a pure and transparent fountain, and there Cyprianus [a martyr who in reality had already died] took a phial which lay at the edge of the fountain and drank; then replenishing it anew, he handed it to me and I drank with joy and, as I said, *"Deo gracias,"* I awoke at the sound of my own voice.

Water, as Jung says, "is an excellent symbol for the living power of the psyche."[50] It is also spiritual and as such is often of a fiery nature.

---

[48] Berthelot, ed., *Collection des Anciens Alchemistes Grecs,* vol. 2, p. 297.

[49] See Scott, ed., *Hermetica,* vol. 1, pp. 149ff.; also *Psychology and Alchemy,* CW 12, pars. 408f.

[50] *Psychology and Alchemy,* CW 12, par. 94.

Figure 6. Alchemical image of the fountain of life.
*(Rosarium philosophorum,* 1550)

The quickening influx of energy from the unconscious may well be looked upon as the effect of the Christian faith, and the water of the *piscina* is here an intimation of a kind of baptismal water, a symbol of Christ or of the Holy Ghost. Thus, for instance, Justin Martyr says:

> As a spring of living water from God, in the land of the heathen barren of all knowledge of God, has this Christ gushed forth, who appeared also to your people, and healed them that from their birth and in the flesh were blind, dumb and lame. . . . Also he awoke the dead. . . . This he did in order to convince those are ready to believe in him that, even if a man be afflicted with any bodily infirmity and yet keeps the commandments given by Christ, he shall be awakened at the second coming with an un-crippled body, after Christ has made him immortal and incorruptible and without sorrow.[51]

In the first Dinocrates dream, Perpetua had felt herself to be inwardly cut off from this living spiritual effect of the Christian teaching, entangled in unconsciousness and overpowered by the weight of outer events. But the following dream—her third vision—which she had in prison shortly before her death, shows her little brother cured of his ills and happy, playing in the Beyond.

This clearly implies that in the meantime, as a result of her intercession—that is, through being consciously concerned with the problem which Dinocrates embodies—she has grown both inward and upward; she has attained an attitude in which the Christian truth becomes a real inner source of strength, and in which her childlike side also actively participates. At the same time, this effect must be understood as an unconscious one, for it proceeds from the Beyond (depicted as Paradise or the Underworld).

Between the first Dinocrates vision and the preceding one, there is indeed no outward connection of motifs, but the inner structure certainly reveals a very striking parallel. This is an important argument in

---

[51] Quoted by Jung in ibid., par. 475, note 141.

support of the fact that we are dealing with a genuine series of dreams and not with a fabrication. In both visions an obstructing element comes into play: in the first, the dragon, as the reaction of the instincts; in the second, Dinocrates, representing Perpetua's own childishness.

In both cases it is a matter of reaching something higher: the ascent of the ladder to an extramundane place, and Dinocrates reaching up to the *piscina* which is too high for him. Both visions depict the attainment of a symbol of the living spirit, and communion with it by means of the milk as heavenly food and through the draught from the fountain of life. Finally, in both the second and third visions there is an allusion to rebirth: on the one hand, in the partaking of milk as food of the reborn; and on the other, in a dramatization of the process in the figure of little Dinocrates who goes off to play "as children do."

Although the problem has undoubtedly come somewhat nearer to the dreamer's consciousness in the second vision. through being connected with a personal content (Dinocrates), Perpetua still projects the inner conflict into the figure of her pagan little brother, from whom, the vision says, she is separated by "a great distance." This means that consciously she is far removed from its realization. In the third vision, however, she is quite personally and actively drawn into the problem. (It may be argued that in the first vision she also played an active part, but there the dream only pointed to the path she was beginning to follow, and there was no actual drama.)

Perpetua's fourth and last vision begins with her in prison, waiting to appear before the beasts. At first sight this is simply a statement of the dreamer's conscious situation. By this the dream implies that the ensuing conflict, depicted in the course of the vision, is actual reality. Nevertheless we are bound to look upon this imprisonment, figuring among the events of the dream, as referring to an inner situation.

In the mysteries of Isis and Serapes there existed a curious custom, that of the so-called *katochoi* (prisoners) of the Deity. *Katoche* principally means arrest or imprisonment, and consequently *katochos* means prisoner. On the other hand, however, the verb *katechesthai ek theou* (used in conjunction with *theophoreisthai* or *korybantian* and with the idea of Bacchic ecstasy) denotes a condition of ecstatic raving; *katochos* then similarly means possessed by a god, and *katoche* a state of possession. (Compare Perpetua's state of trance during her martyrdom.)

Such *katochoi* existed as early as the second century before Christ, for instance in the Serapium of Memphis, a sect in which the state of imprisonment was one of free choice to which laymen voluntarily submitted, as novitiates, prior to their initiation into the priesthood. The *katochoi* also called themselves "slaves" or "servants of God." Some of them even wore chains and often did not leave the outer court of the temple for years. Others went about begging and lived a life of the most rigorous self-imposed asceticism. Many of them interpreted their own dreams and took them very seriously. Their period of imprisonment often lasted till such a time as the novice and an already-initiated mystic had the same dream on the same night. This would admit the novice to initiation. It might occur suddenly, or after waiting many years, or sometimes never. The novice also occasionally chose the spiritual father who initiated him.[52] Whoever attempted initiation without being "called" was doomed to die. And only the man whom Isis had appointed in a dream might enter the *adyton* of the goddess.

All these ancient customs may undoubtedly be looked upon as the first steps leading to the Christian institution of monachism which originated in Egypt.[53] It is also noteworthy that St. Paul should speak of himself as "a prisoner *[desmios]* of Jesus Christ" (Eph. 3:1) or of being "in the bonds of the Gospel."

The psychological meaning of such a confinement is unmistakable. Imprisonment under whatever circumstances implies restricted freedom of action and isolation from the surrounding world. It is a sequestration, a voluntary or involuntary state of introversion, which in certain cases may be brought about by a state of possession—that is, by being fascinated with an unconscious content. This is how the unconscious images (therefore the dreams) which formed the initiation process of the mysteries were activated. That is why the prison is often an initial symbol of the process of individuation in contemporary dreams.

In the ancient mysteries the initiation took place under the guidance of a spiritual leader. On parallel lines, in Perpetua's vision, the deacon Pomponius knocks at the prison door. He wears a festive garment and manifold shoes. He takes her by the hand and leads her through dark and devious paths to the arena.

At that time, a deacon was an assistant to the bishop in his diocese, a kind of parochial aide. Here we are dealing with a real personality known to Perpetua. By means of bribery he was able to bring about

---

[52] See Reitzenstein, *Historische Monachism und Historische Lausiaca,* pp. 107ff.

[53] [Monachism, according to the American Heritage Dictionary, is an archaic term for monasticism.—Ed.]

some alleviation in the conditions of her captivity, and he was also a spiritual support to her. In the dream, Pomponius has evidently taken upon himself the function of a Christian animus figure (which is natural, seeing that Perpetua, who had been baptized only twenty days before, in all probability projected her Christian attitude onto the deacon of the place). He is now the leader of her soul (he takes her by the hand) and her spiritual father, a symbol of her Christian faith.

The function that Pomponius fulfills is similar to that of Saturus in the first vision. Should there be any difference in their roles, it would mainly consist in the fact that Saturus seems rather to embody her temperamentally courageous inner attitude in the face of her martyrdom, whereas Pomponius is more of a teacher—that is to say, he stands more for the Christian faith as a spiritual doctrine.[54] In the dream he is characterized as one who is already initiated (which clearly does not reflect his position in real life and proves the projection): he wears a festive garment and manifold shoes.

In the ancient mysteries the festive garment plays an important role, as the celestial garment of the glorified celestial body, which the mystic puts on. Thus, before his third initiation, Apuleius was exhorted in a dream to be initiated anew in order to attain further enlightenment, as he could no longer wear "the garment of the Goddess which he had put on in the province and had then laid aside in the sanctuary there."[55] In Egypt the resurrected one wore the headdress of the sun-god Ra, a sun-diadem. The Mithraic mystics received a garment on which animals were embroidered. It signified the glorified resurrection after death, the state of full enlightenment through the Gnosis and of becoming one with the Deity; at the same time it meant a *metasomatosis,* a complete transformation.

In the Christian concept of Paradise, the Blessed are robed in

---

[54] See Emma Jung, *Animus and Anima,* pp. 5ff.

[55] Apuleius, *Metamorphosis,* XI. [For English, see W. Adlington, trans., *The Golden Ass of Apuleius,* pp. 299f.—Ed.]

white—as a symbol of joy and innocence, according to one of the Fathers of the Church. Here the deacon Pomponius is likewise an already fully enlightened mystic, a spirit from the Beyond—that is, a
figure arising from the unconscious. At the same time he is a symbol
of Perpetua's own coming development. He says: "Perpetua, we are
awaiting thee, come!" From the World Beyond, Paradise or the land
of the dead, he brings her the message that they are expecting her
there. He is also the one whose office it is to usher her into this place.

   The animus is indeed the figure that transmits the contents of the
collective unconscious; he is a psychopomp. The words he addresses
to her in the amphitheater where he leaves her ("Fear not, I am here
with thee and shall fight with thee") show that he stands much less for
a concrete figure than for an unconscious, spiritual power. In the
dream, however, he disappears, and in his place enters a gigantic *lanista* who promises her the bough of the Tree of Life if she wins the
battle. Thus, in the function he fulfills, he evolves, as it were, into
this bigger, more archetypal figure which (as we shall see) is clearly a
symbol of both an absolute faith and a positive attitude.

   At first Pomponius leads Perpetua through a rough and pathless
country, and it is only with great effort that they reach the amphitheater. Such straying about on tortuous paths recalls the plight of her
little brother Dinocrates in Hades, described in her second vision. A
disorientation has obviously set in at this point, a condition of per-
plexity and distress resulting from the state of introversion symbolized by the prison. Perpetua is evidently assailed by doubts and resis-
tances at the thought of her martyrdom. In the midst of this disorientation of her consciousness, the deacon becomes her guiding Christian
animus—that is to say, a symbol of the Christian faith.

   Pomponius takes her to the amphitheater/arena. Its shape recalls a
magic circle or mandala. As a symbol of the Self, which embraces the
totality of the conscious and unconscious sides of the psyche, the amphitheater naturally includes both the opposing attitudes and the con-

scious portion of the personality. These are personified by the pagan Egyptian and the Christian assistants and by Perpetua herself, with the *lanista* symbolizing the value of the Self.

In the ritual mandala, the circular boundary surrounding the center always has the purpose of preventing an outburst or a disintegration, as well as preventing any interference from the outside. It is inside this enclosure that the final contest now takes place. Inasmuch as the ritual mandala also aims at reconciling the opposites, the very appearance of this symbol is already an intimation of a possible solution of the conflict. This doubtless consists in the fact that Perpetua will be "withdrawn" into the suprapersonal meaning of the process to such a degree (compare her trance during her martyrdom) that she will be able to endure the destruction of her individual existence.

Historically, the amphitheater was actually a circular building devoted to a cult, and the games that took place there were religious ceremonies in honor of the gods. Therefore Tertullian rightly called it "the *temple* of all demons."[56] It is here that the crowd in the vision now gathers to witness the fight between the Saint and the Egyptian. One might say that the Christian inner guiding principle leads to a concentration of the conflict in Perpetua herself, around which stand the formerly dissociated forces of the collective unconscious (the people. All the various parts of the personality collect around a suprapersonal center, where the final conflict between the opposites will be decided.

At first Perpetua expects the wild beasts to be let in. Interpreted on the subjective level, this means that she believes the fight is to be waged against the unconscious in the form of the animal world of the instincts. These are the same forces she has already encountered in the guise of the dragon. But the dream shows that, in reality, the conflict is far more complicated: a gigantic Egyptian of horrible appear-

---

[56] Tertullian, *de Spectaculis,* 12. [For English, see Roberts and Donaldson, eds, *Ante-Nicene Fathers,* vol. 3.—Ed.]

ance comes toward her with a sword.

This Egyptian is a remarkably complex embodiment of her situation. In late antiquity Egypt meant the land of ancient wisdom. It was looked on in much the same way that the modern European looks upon India. As far back as Herodotus, Egypt and her priests held this meaning. Plato, for example, was wont to give out his most important ideas and myths as the secret wisdom of the Egyptian priesthood. According to Hekataios of Miletus, the Egyptians were the oldest and most religious people in the whole world.

The Greeks projected their own unconscious onto Egypt, and as a result it became the source of all secret revelation, the land where an archaic religious attitude was still to be found, which their own enlightened consciousness had lost. Thus, in a satire, Apuleius's Lucian (whom we know also from Apuleius's *Golden Ass*) says:

> The oldest philosophers were the Hindu Brahmans, or Gymnosophists. Philosophy went direct from them to the Ethiopians, from thence to the Egyptians.[57]

The Cynics especially saw the realization of their ideals in these Indian and Egyptian sages. Egypt was therefore the site par excellence of all dark magic, and the cult of the animal that was practiced there made a particularly deep impression upon the Greek philosophers and sophists. In the "Treatise Asclepius III" of the *Corpus Hermeticum*, Hermes says:

> Do you know, Asclepius, that Egypt is an image of heaven, or, to speak more exactly, in Egypt all the operations and powers which rule and work in heaven have been transferred to earth below? Nay, it should rather be said that the *whole Kosmos dwells in this our land* [Egypt] *as in its sanctuary*.[58]

---

[57] See Reitzenstein, *Hellenistiche Wunderzählungen*, pp. 41ff.
[58] Scott, ed., *Hermetica*, vol. 1, pp. 340f.

If the pagans thus looked to Egypt as the land of the great mysteries, the most religious land of ancient wisdom and magic, in the eyes of the Christians it was bound to become the prototype of all that was evil, and especially of the "clouded, obscure, misleading Pagan spirit."[59]

For the Gnostic Perates, however, Egypt also meant the transitory world, the passage through the Red Sea, the way to immortality. In their allegorical interpretation of the Bible, the Fathers of the Church very soon explained the exodus of the Israelites from Egypt as an exodus out of spiritual darkness. (Such things can hardly have been unknown to Perpetua, who came of an educated family.)

In a certain sense the Egyptian in Perpetua's fourth vision also constitutes an analogy to the dragon in the first vision, since both—as Hugo Rahner so beautifully demonstrates[60]—became images of the devil in the patristic symbolic language. The Fathers of the Church found support for this in the passages in Ezekiel where God causes the Egyptian Pharaoh to be addressed as "the great dragon that lieth in the midst of his rivers" (29:3), and "as a whale [dragon] in the seas" (32:2). Thus the Egyptian king (drowned in the Red Sea) also becomes an image of the devil.

From the psychological point of view, on the other hand, there is a difference between the image of the devil as dragon and as Egyptian, inasmuch as the latter embodies a more spiritual content which is closer to consciousness. Accordingly, Perpetua's fourth vision reveals that the central conflict does not consist solely in overcoming the animal instincts but also implies a fight against the spirit of paganism, against the experience of the spirit projected into nature, against the spirit of the most ancient tradition and against the spirit of the earth from which the Christians endeavored to free themselves.

In this connection the four visions show a gradual development of

[59] Ibid.

[60] Rahner, "Antemna Crucis II," in *Zeitschrift für Kathol. Theologie*, p. 111.

the pagan counterattitude in the unconscious: at first it is embodied in a lower, cold-blooded animal (the dragon); then it appears in human form, as an ill child (Dinocrates); and lastly as a full-grown warrior (the Egyptian). So the conflict is continuously being brought nearer to consciousness, and at the same time the menacing factor grows increasingly important, appearing in ever more spiritual terms. It is in this last form that paganism proved most dangerous to the Christian faith. Therefore St. Paul says:

> Put on the whole armor of God, that ye may be able to stand against the wiles of the devil.
>
> For we wrestle not against flesh and blood, but against principalities, against powers [*archas kai exousias,* i.e., the domination of the spirits of the planets], against the rulers of the darkness of this world, against spiritual wickedness in high places [*pros ta pneumatika tes ponerias en tois epouraniois].* (Eph. 6:11-12)

By this he means the *pneuma* projected into the cosmos and into nature, the pagan experience of the spirit.

The Christian devil is in truth none other than the *Agathodaimon* of the pagans, once worshipped as lord of the black Egyptian earth and husband of Isis. Referring to this scene, we also read in a sermon ascribed to St. Augustine: "How art thou fallen from heaven, O Lucifer, son of the morning!" (Isa. 14:12) This is clearly an allusion to the bright, spiritual side of this divine opponent of Christ.

The fact that the Egyptian in Perpetua's vision wallows in the dust, and that Perpetua, as she conquers him, treads him into the earth, stresses precisely the earthly quality, the state of being imprisoned in the earth, which is characteristic of this *pneuma.*[61] According to Philo of Alexandria, the kingdom of the air, against whose demons St.

---

[61] See Tertullian, *de Pallio,* 3. (For English, see Roberts and Donaldson, eds., *Ante-Nicene Fathers,* vol. 3.) Rolling in the dust is also a trick that the wrestler uses in order to make it difficult for his opponent to lay hold of him.

Paul fights, is black;[62] and in the *Epistle of Barnabas* (IV:10, XX:1)
the devil is already called the black one. Besides this, the blackness of
the Egyptians—and particularly of the priests of Isis who were im-
ported into Rome to celebrate the mysteries and whose dark com-
plexions were singularly striking there—strengthened the conception
of the devil as an Egyptian, a symbol of the dark, chthonic mysteries
of departing antiquity.

In the event of defeat, Perpetua was to be killed by the sword of
the Egyptian. But it is she who conquers him and then treads on his
head, which again points to the mental function of this enemy. During the fight he endeavors to lay hold of her feet. Psychologically,
this means that he is seeking to undermine her standpoint, to make
her doubt her convictions and thus cause her to waver. A passage in
the writings of Origen, who calls the pagan attitude a "spiritual Ethiopian," also points to the character of this dark Egyptian, who is as the
same time a figure parallel to the serpent:

> He who partakes of the supernatural bread, and strengthens his heart
> thereby, will become the son of God. But he who partakes of the dragon
> is himself no other than the spiritual Ethiopian, in that by the snares laid
> for the dragon, he is himself transformed into the serpent.[63]

(Perpetua treads on the Egyptian's head, just as in the first vision
she stepped on the head of the dragon.)

When the Egyptian throws himself at Perpetua's feet, the dream
seems to suggest a connection with Perpetua's father. The latter
never ceased to pursue her with entreaties to recant her Christian
faith, and his exhortations appear to have affected her deeply, for
upon one occasion she said: "I thank God, and recovered when he had

---

[62] *De Opificio Mundi,* 7.29. (For English, see F.H. Colson and G.H. Whitaker, eds.,
*Philo with an English translation.)*

[63] Origen, *Peri euches,* 27:12. (For English, see Roberts and Donaldson, eds., *Ante-
Nicene Fathers.)*

departed."[64] Among the many arguments he used, he once pleaded with her as follows:

> Daughter . . . have pity on my grey head—have pity on me your father, if
> I deserve to be called your father, if I have favoured you above all your
> brothers, if I have raised you to reach this prime of your life. Do not
> abandon me to be the reproach of men. Think of your brothers, think of
> your mother and your aunt, think of your child, who will not be able to
> live once you are gone. Give up your pride! You will destroy all of us!
> None of us will ever be able to speak freely again if anything happens to
> you.[65]

Perpetua goes on to say:

> This was the way my father spoke out of love for me, kissing my hands
> and throwing himself down before me. With tears in his eyes he no longer
> addressed me as his daughter but as a woman *[domina]*. I was sorry for
> my father's sake, because he alone of all my kin would be unhappy to see
> me suffer. [66]

This moving passage sheds a profound light on the way her family affected Perpetua's fate. Her relation to her father appears to have been a particularly close one. In the case of a woman, the father stands for the first image of man in general, the first embodiment of the animus, and as such he determines her spiritual temperament and her relation to spiritual contents generally. Therefore, through her relation to her father, Perpetua seems to have been in great measure fated to suffer the conflict and to come to terms with the religious problems of her day.

Perpetua's father, on the other hand, appears to have been just as unusually attached to her. (He addresses her "as a woman." On one occasion, when she turns a deaf ear to his entreaties, he falls upon her,

---

[64] Musurillo, trans., "Perpetua," in *Acts of the Christian Martyrs,* p. 112.

[65] Ibid., p. 113.

[66] Ibid.

screaming, and moves as if to tear her eyes out. Since Perpetua is very closely bound to him, his arguments against Christianity wound her very deeply. Once, when he leaves her after a scene such as the one just described, she says that "he departed, vanquished along with his diabolical arguments *[cum argumentis diabolis].*"[67]

So there is some justification for drawing a certain psychological parallel between the Egyptian who throws himself at Perpetua's feet and upon whom she looks as the devil, and the figure of her father.

St. Augustine likewise recognizes this connection and therefore says that the devil made use of the father, instructing him with deceiving words in order to bring about Perpetua's downfall by appealing to her feeling of filial piety. It is the spirit of her father—that is, the spirit of tradition—in Perpetua herself which rebels against the new creed. When the dream substitutes the more general figure of the Egyptian for that of the father, it expresses the fact that the fight is not only against the individual father, but against that which he means to Perpetua in an inner sense: a fight against a universal spirit, a pagan animus, which must be overcome. The Egyptian's threat is to pierce her with his sword—that is, to enter her, penetrate her spiritually; and when he throws himself at her feet it is not with the intention of entreating her, as in the case of her real father, but of bringing about her fall, of destroying her standpoint.

Then, in the fourth vision, Perpetua is surrounded by fair youths who befriend her; they unclothe her and massage her body with oil, as for a Greek *agon* (contest). And she is transformed into a man.

This unveiling of her masculine nature, so to speak, at this particular time, appears to be in some measure connected with personal considerations. About the year 200 A.D., the persecutions of the Christians in Africa were of a local character and very much encouraged by the aggressive attitude of the Christians themselves. Perpetua,

---

[67] Ibid., p. 108.

as a young woman of twenty-two with a tiny son, would hardly have had to suffer such a fate had she not adopted the strong, masculine spirit of the believer and thrown herself actively into the spiritual battle. It is also obvious that she sought a martyr's death to demonstrate her faith, as is shown by her remark at the time of her baptism:

> I was inspired by the Spirit not to ask for any other favor after the [baptismal] water but simply the perseverance [sufferings] of the flesh.[68]

Perhaps one may therefore be justified in looking upon her prison *(katoche)* as a state of possession. In any case the dream shows that in the conflict which now breaks out she adopts a masculine, warlike attitude and identifies completely with the Christian animus figures that had appeared only as unconscious parts of her personality in the earlier dreams. She becomes a *miles Christi,* a soldier of Christ, just as also in the pagan world the initiation into the mysteries was frequently interpreted as a *sacramentum* (military oath). In the mysteries of Mithras, for instance, the initiates of a certain degree were called *milites* (soldiers). Their service was a military service dedicated to the God, and the Pauline conception of the *militia Christi* likewise grew out of these ideas. St. Paul describes himself as a *stratiotes* (soldier) and speaks of the "armor of light." (Rom. 13:12}

But the laying off of Perpetua's garment has a still deeper meaning. In the *Corpus Hermeticum* we read:

> Seek for yourselves one who, holding you by the hand, leads the way [here it is Pomponius] to the gates of the Gnosis, where the shining light, clear of all darkness, is to be found; where no one is ever drunk, but where all are sober, looking into their hearts toward Him who wishes to be seen. For He cannot be heard, nor read, nor yet is He visible to the eyes, but only to the spirit and the heart.
>
> First, however, thou must rend the garment which thou wearest, the web of unconsciousness *[to hyphasma tes agnosias],* the stronghold of

---

[68] Ibid., p. 109.

wickedness, the bonds which thou bearest, the dark veil, the living death, the visible corpse, the surrounding grave . . . . [For this is] the hostile garment, which narrows thee down to thyself, so that thou canst not raise thine eyes above to the beauty of truth.[69]

Therefore, in order for the mystic in this initiation to receive the glorified celestial garment of light, he must first remove and tear up his garment of earthly materialness *(soma—sema)* and the *agnosia* (unconsciousness).

In the apocryphal *Odes of Solomon,* which were influenced by Gnosticism, we likewise read:

I forsook the folly which is cast over the earth; and I stripped it off and cast it from me: and the Lord renewed me in His raiment, and possessed me by His light.[70]

And further: "I put off darkness and clothed myself with light."[71] And again: "I was clothed with the covering of thy Spirit, and thou didst remove from me my raiment of skins."[72]

So this laying aside of the garment means stripping away unconscious animal nature, the state of imprisonment in illusion and, under certain conditions, even earthly material existence. Thus, Perpetua becomes, so to speak, entirely a spirit (hence her masculinity).

In the *Excerpta ex Theodoto,* quoted by Clement of Alexandria, we likewise read that the masculine always unites directly with Logos, but that the feminine, after a process of becoming masculine, enters the *Pleroma* together with the angels. That is why it is said that woman is transformed into man and the earthly Church into angels.[73] This means the redemption of the "psychical" through its transformation

---

[69] Scott, ed., *Hermetica,* VII, S 2, 3.

[70] Bernard, ed., *Odes of Solomon,* Ode 11.

[71] Ibid., Ode 21.

[72] Ibid., Ode 25.

[73] See Robinson, "The Fragments of Heracleon" in *Texts and Studies,* 1:57, note 28.

into the "pneumatical." The belief that in the Beyond the sexes cease to exist as opposites and are united is also alluded to in a *logion* transmitted by Clement of Alexandria:

> When ye shall have trodden underfoot the cloak of shame [compare the laying aside of Perpetua's garment] and when the two will have become one, and the outer like the inner, and the masculine like the feminine, neither masculine nor feminine.[74]

This idea is based on the supposition that the two sexes are united within the human being not only physiologically but also as a psychological totality, seeing that the unconscious invariably contains the opposite qualities of each individual. Hence, in Hermetic philosophy, the hermaphrodite becomes the symbol of totality (see Figure 7, opposite).

In Perpetua's case, however, it is not a union of opposites that takes place, but an inversion, which corresponds to a complete extinction of the previous ego-consciousness, in place of which, in the state of ecstasy, there appears another spiritual consciousness.

The extent to which St. Augustine intuitively grasped these psychological facts and expressed them in the language of his time is almost unbelievable. Referring to Ephesians 4:13 ("Till we all come in the unity of the faith, and of the knowledge of the Son of God, unto a perfect man . . ." and so on), Augustine says that because the devil "felt himself to be in the presence of a woman who behaved to him like a man" *(viriliter secum agentem feminam sensit),*[75] he determined to tempt her by means of a man, choosing for this purpose her father, who besieged her with his arguments. And in *de Anima* he even adds:

> In a dream, Perpetua saw herself *changed into a man,* fighting with an Egyptian. Who, however, can doubt that it was her soul that appeared in this [masculine] bodily form, not her actual body, which latter, having

---

[74] *Stromata* III, 13.92.

[75] See C.J.M.J. van Beek, *Passio Sanctarum Perpetuae et Felicitatis,* p. 155.

Figure 7. Hermaphrodite on the winged globe of chaos.
(Jamsthaler, *Viatorium spagyricum,* 1625)

> remained completely feminine, lay unconscious, whereas *her soul* fought in the aforesaid form of a masculine body.[76]

In effect, she becomes identical with the animus. The Montanist prophetess Maximilla provides another striking parallel when, in her prophecies inspired by the Spirit, she speaks of herself in the masculine form.

Inasmuch as the Christian symbols rose to the light of day as a new and creative content coming from the depths of the collective unconscious, the people of that time were drawn into the unconscious by them. In Perpetua's case too, the Christian symbols appear in the unconscious (the shepherd in the Beyond and the fountain of life in the underworld). The conflict is not one between a consciousness newly converted to Christianity and the still-pagan unconscious; on the contrary, the Christian symbol itself also appears in the unconscious, and it is there that the opposites clash. The same phenomenon occurs in a reversed form in the case of the author of the *Shepherd of Hermas:* thanks to a woman, to his meeting with the anima, he is initiated into a new doctrine.

This whole period of evolution, when the Christian world was coming into being, is characterized by a powerful influx of the collective unconscious. Miracles were in the air; and in the catacomb pictures, the people of that time wear a peculiarly eager expression, their glance directed inward, as though they expected something tremendously fascinating to emerge from that direction.

The young men in the dream who anoint Perpetua with oil after her transformation are helpful figures like Pomponius, but they are split up into a plurality—a typical characteristic of an animus figure.

Oil, especially in the form of scented ointment *(unguentum),* plays an important role in all primitive rites. It is a fluid charged with power and is a means of healing, of beautifying, of preserving the dead and

---

[76] IV: 18, 26.

so on. The ancient images of the gods were also anointed with oil in order to bring them to life. The Roman Catholic Church likewise uses scented oil *(myron)* which has been consecrated by the priest, especially in the case of extreme unction, to impart spiritual strength. Thus Cyrillus, a Father of the Church, says:

> The oil which has been consecrated by the priest is no longer mere oil, but in the same way as the bread becomes the body of Christ, the oil becomes the *charisma* of Christ and of the Holy Ghost in an energized form *[energetikon charisma].*[77]

In other words, it becomes the archetype of the Holy Ghost, who was frequently thought of as a nourishing, satisfying perfume. Therefore oil also meant Gnosis. Honorius of Autun says: "Naked of all vices and anointed with the oil of the *charisma,* must we fight the devil!"[78] So here likewise the laying aside of the garment is a laying aside of vices, of the *agnosia* or unconsciousness.

Moreover, this passage in the vision bears a close resemblance to a part of the Slavonic *Book of Enoch* (22:8): before entering into the highest Heaven, Enoch is divested of his earthly garments by the angel Michael, anointed with fine oil, and arrayed in the garment of God's majesty.[79] This ointment "resembled a great light . . . and shone like the rays of the sun." According to the rules of the Church established by Hippolytus, the catechumens were also anointed by the bishop with the laying on of hands as a transmission of the spirit.

So this anointing with oil means a spiritual strengthening and enlightening by means of these animus figures. (In the Greek text they appear as a youth who sends forth flashes of lightning, and other fair youths. To send forth lightning means to enlighten.) These unite to form the figure of the giant *lanista.* He is of such enormous size that

---

[77] Migne, ed., *Patrologiae,* Greek series, vol. 30, col. 1089.

[78] Ibid., Latin series, vol. 172, col. 857.

[79] See W.R. Morfill, ed., and R.H. Charles, trans., *The Book of the Secrets of Enoch.*

he almost towers above the whole amphitheater. He carries a rod or staff in one hand, and in the other a green bough bearing golden apples which he promises to Perpetua as a reward of victory. Like Pomponius, he has a loose toga with a broad purple stripe across the middle of his chest between two others, and he wears "manifold shoes made of gold and silver." Since Pomponius promised to help Perpetua, we may assume that he has, as it were, been transformed into the *lanista,* or at least that he was an early form of this figure.

The staff is evidently a sign that this daimon is also a guide. The staff is generally associated with Hermes, messenger of the gods and leader of souls; it is a golden rod which is similar to the magic wand of the magician. The shepherd-deity likewise carries a staff and shares with the *lanista* the characteristic of supernatural size. At bottom, it is the same figure. The staff gives him the quality of a guiding and judging principle. Honorius of Autun, for instance, interpreted the bishop's staff as *auctoritas doctrinae* (the authority of the doctrine).[80] The staff characterizes the *lanista* as a personification of the right faith, the *pistis*—that is, the personification of a guiding principle which will settle the conflict and be the absolute judge of the life and death of the soul.

Judging also plays a remarkable role with St. Paul. According to him, "He that is spiritual [the *pneumatikoi*] judgeth all things, yet he himself is judged of no man." (1 Cor. 2:15) This absolute infallibility of the *pneumatikoi* is based on the fact that he possesses, so to speak, the mind *(Nous)* of Christ, and the *Nous* of God judges absolutely. In the *Magic Papyri,* as we saw earlier, the Egyptian *Agathodaimon* is addressed as "thou who sittest on the head of the cosmos, and judgest everything, surrounded by the circle of truth and faith."[81] On the last day Christ will also appear as such a judge of the world.

Thus the *lanista* carries the symbol of unshakable faith which defi-

---

[80] Migne, ed., *Patrologiae,* Latin series, vol. 172, col. 610.

[81] See above, pp. 40f.

nitely settles the conflict. In this sense, he is truly the "spirit of truth" which "shall be with you." In the presence of such an inviolable faith, every human criterion comes to an end: the individual is enabled to suffer even death willingly for its sake.

The gold and silver shoes of the *lanista* point to an analogous psychic factor. As an aspect of clothing that mirrors one's attitude to one's surroundings, one's standpoint, shoes stand for a component of our inner attitude which is especially concerned with the earth—that is, with reality. In this sense shoes might be looked upon as representing how one relates to earthly things. The German saying, "to lay aside children's shoes," for instance, means to outgrow an infantile attitude toward reality. In folklore shoes often have an erotic meaning, particularly as the feminine, receptive principle. That they are also a symbol of power is perhaps most clearly expressed in the expression, "to be completely under someone's heel."

The shoes of the *lanista* thus symbolize a psychic attitude which is receptive to reality, and at the same time they express unshakable steadfastness. They show that he not only embodies a directing principle but also bestows a standpoint both incorruptible and secure.

In addition, the *lanista* wears a white garment with three purple stripes across the chest. According to Shewring, this means that a purple undergarment was visible between the two end stripes of the toga.[82] White and red are the colors of the priests of the African Saturn and of the Egyptian mysteries in general, and in alchemy they represent the two highest stages—the *albedo* and *rubedo*. (Here the equivalent of the alchemical *nigredo* appears separately in the form of the Egyptian.) White indicates the first transfiguration in alchemy, and also the dominance of the feminine principle; red implies the dominance of the masculine principle and is the color of the new Sun King. According to Mithraic texts also, the god Helios wears a white

---

[82] See *The Passion of SS. Perpetua and Felicity*, p. 109.

garment and a scarlet mantle.

Therefore the garment of the *lanista* contains an allusion to the highest stages of initiation into the mysteries, and also to the reconciliation of the opposites in the unconscious. The presence of the three red stripes might point to the fact that here an upper triad has detached itself from a lower fourth element. A higher triad has appeared in opposition to the dark power represented by the Egyptian, which in alchemy, for instance, was looked upon as the fourth factor and the foundation of a uniform development.[83] The dark *prima materia* was frequently described in alchemy as *caput draconis* (dragon's head), or as *draco,* whose head represented man as the *vita gloriosa* to which the angels minister. The *prima materia* was also occasionally portrayed as an Ethiopian.

The vision of one of the martyrs in the "Passio Mariani et Jacobi" provides a strikingly close parallel to the *lanista:*

> I saw a youth of incredibly gigantic stature, whose loose garment shone with such a bright light, that our eyes could not dwell on it. His feet did not touch the ground and his countenance was above the clouds.
>
> As he hastened past us, he threw us each—into thy lap, Marianus, and into mine—a purple girdle, and spake: "Follow me!"

The martyrs interpret this apparition as Christ. According to the "Apocalypse of Peter," also, the bodies of the righteous "were whiter than snow and redder than any rose, and the red thereof was mingled with the white."[84]

Thus the conflict in the middle of the magic circle which Perpetua has reached reveals itself as a clash between two suprapersonal, spiritual powers: the Egyptian as the spirit of paganism, of the *pneuma*

---

[83] See *Scriptum Alberti super arborem Aristotelis,* in *Theatrum Chemicum,* vol. 2, p. 525.

[84] A. Dietrich, *Nekyia,* pp. 3f.; see also "The Revelation of Peter," in M.R. James, ed., *Two Lectures on the Newly Discovered Fragments, etc.,* p. 46.

projected into the cosmos, and a new spiritual power which confronts him, tending entirely in the opposite direction, toward the Beyond, and laying claim to the absolute truth. But this spirit is nevertheless also a *kosmokrator* and *pneuma* which reaches from heaven to earth. Like the lord of the Egyptian earth it is also an *Agathodaimon* and a shepherd of men.

Indeed, perhaps the most singular feature in Perpetua's fourth vision is that, when one probes deeply into the conflicting, opposite principles, one is confronted with their peculiar similarity. This comes from the fact that they are both in the unconscious.

It is really astounding that the spiritual power which has the casting vote in this conflict should be personified by a figure belonging most unmistakably to the pagan world, the trainer of gladiators, and not by a Christian figure such as Saturus or Pomponius, for instance, or Christ himself. This can only be explained by the fact that the unconscious as a whole, in its still pagan aspect, was actually working to build up a Christian consciousness. Hence, to be a Christian in those days meant unconditional obedience to the inner voice.

We might also say that had Christ appeared as the *lanista,* he would have been taking sides in the fight, so to speak. But the decisive factor which desired Perpetua's victory was the Self in a form which showed itself to be beyond the opposites, *Christus et eius umbra.* The non-Christian nature of the *lanista* is again expressed in a significant detail—in his garment. His garment, with the peculiarly broad purple stripes on the toga and the scarlet undergarment, is very similar to that worn by the African priests of Saturn, who was especially honored as a god of vegetation and of the underworld. Thus, it represented the very Deity against whom the Christians had to fight the hardest battle. Saturn was looked upon as the special tutelary god of animal fights[85]—so that he was also a *lanista* and umpire par excel-

---

[85] See Lactantius Firmianus, *Divinarum Institutionum Libri Septum,* vol. 6, p. 20. [For English see Roberts and Donaldson, eds., *Ante-Nicene Fathers,* vol. 7.—Ed.]

lence—the spirit of the amphitheater. One could almost fancy that it was this spirit which appeared to Perpetua as the *lanista*.

It is remarkable how similar the images and texts of budding Christianity were to those of the Gnostic and pagan mysteries which it fought against with such ardor. Indeed, the Fathers of the Church themselves who inveighed against paganism were not blind to this fact and could only explain it as a subtle *diabolica fraus*. The then widespread conception of a *Daimon Antimimos* (hostile and mimicking) who stands in the Redeemer's way was doubtlessly founded on such facts. For instance, Zosimos says:

> [Christ] appeared to the very feeble as a man capable of suffering and like one scourged. And after he had privily stolen away the Men of Light that were his own, he made known that in truth he did not suffer, and that death was trampled down and cast out. . . . Thus they [the men of light] kill their Adam. And these things are so until the coming of the daemon Antimimos, the jealous one, who seeks to lead them astray as before, declaring that he is the Son of God, although he is formless *[amorphos]* in both body and soul.[86]

Curiously enough, the Poimandres of the *Corpus Hermeticum* is opposed by a similar "fire-breathing" daimon of vengeance and punishment, a similar power of destiny.[87] We meet the same idea when St. Paul draws a comparison between the first "earthy" *(choikos)* Adam and the second Adam, who is "a quickening spirit" *(pneuma zoopoion)*. And lastly, this opposition appears also in the idea of the Antichrist.

Perpetua herself does not use the designation *Antimimos* but simply calls the Egyptian *diabolus;* yet he possesses this peculiar quality of an antigod in matter, a nature-spirit which, while aping the Christian

---

[86] Berthelot, ed., *Collection des Anciens Alchemistes Grecs*, vol. 3, p. 49; also quoted by Jung in *Psychology and Alchemy*, CW 12, par. 456. (In the Greek text of the "Passio Perpetua," the Egyptian is likewise called *amorphos.)*

[87] See Scott, ed., *Hermetica*, vol. 13.

spirit, is nevertheless its opponent. If we ask ourselves what is actually taking place autonomously in the collective unconscious, we can perceive a splitting-up, as it were, of the archetype into a light and a dark aspect. This happened first of all to the image of God, inasmuch as the ambivalent, primordial father, Yahweh, approached the human sphere in the form of the two sons, Satan and Christ.[88] This tearing apart of the light and dark aspects of the image of God, as it is described by Jung, is true of all the other symbolic images. In Rhabanus Maurus's list of *figurae,* for instance, nearly all the *typi* (allegorical images), such as fire, eyes and lion, have one aspect which alludes to Christ and another which alludes to the devil.[89]

The split into two aspects of the image of God, and at the same time of all other archetypal images, appears to be connected—as Jung states in his Eranos article on the mother archetype[90]—with the differentiation of feeling and, consequently, with moral judgment in Western culture. This subsequently made it impossible to endure the paradoxical character and moral ambivalence still retained by, for instance, the Indian gods.

However, this moral reaction was preceded and induced by the constellation of the new archetypal situation itself, first revealed in the form of a transcendent psychic presence, as Perpetua's visions show so clearly. Splitting the image of God into *Christus-Diabolus* constellated a problem of the opposites which was to lead to a schism in times to come. The one-sided belief in the light side which characterized the exponents of early Christianity—such as Perpetua—was

---

[88] For a fuller description of this inner divine drama, see various essays by Jung, including "The Spirit Mercurius," *Alchemical Studies,* CW 13; "A Psychological Approach to the Dogma of the Trinity," *Psychology and Religion,* CW 11; and "The Phenomenology of the Spirit in Fairy Tales," *The Archetypes and the Collective Unconscious,* CW 9i.

[89] See Migne, ed., *Patrologiae,* Latin series, vol. 112, cols. 907ff.

[90] "Psychological Aspects of the Mother Archetype," *The Archetypes and the Collective Unconscious,* CW 9i.

bound, in obedience to the law of enantiodromia,[91] to be followed by the problem of the Antichrist, "Lord of This World." This question, however, was only to arise in the second era of the astrological age of Pisces.

It is particularly interesting in the visions of St. Perpetua to be able to observe this splitting-up process in the unconscious psyche itself. An equally remarkable fact is that the *lanista* still incorporates a remnant of the pagan spirit in which the opposites are united, but whose aim is unmistakably to urge humanity to be partisan of the light side.

The daimon who guides Perpetua in the person of the *lanista* carries yet a third attribute, the green bough with the golden fruit. This is a bough from the Tree of Life, a general archetypal image which is to be found all over the world. It is the tree of the Hesperides, whose fruit signifies eternal life. It is also important in alchemy as *arbor solis et lunae.* It is no accident that Perpetua receives this bough at the hands of the leader of souls, for the tree grows in the west, the way of the night sea journey. In the *Aeneid,* before the hero can enter the land of the dead he must break the "golden bough."[92] So the bough is at the same time the promise of eternal life and a means of passing over into the kingdom of the dead, of descending into the unconscious. This vision is particularly impressive when one considers that Perpetua had the dream on the eve of her actual death.

In the *Passio Mariani et Jacobi,* a boy who had been put to death three days before appeared to one of the martyrs, wearing a wreath of roses around his neck and carrying the greenest branch of a palm tree *(palma viridissima)* in his right hand. He tells them that he is feasting merrily and that they will soon eat with him. The bough of the Tree of Life with the golden apples corresponds to the milk in the first vision and to the water of life in the Dinocrates dream. Gold is a symbol

---

[91] [Enantiodromia, literally "running counter to," refers to the emergence of the unconscious opposite in the course of time.—Ed.]

[92] *Aeneid,* Book 6, pp. 140ff.

for the highest value (Dinocrates also drank out of a golden phial). The green bough points to the fact that this highest value is a living element which has grown naturally.

Accordingly, the new spirit which towers above humanity fills Perpetua with absolute and unshakable conviction, and at the same time it transmits to her from the unconscious the highest living value, which one may surely look upon as the Deity. This spirit gives her the inner conviction of God's existence, which makes it easy for her to die. But again, for this very reason, her actual death becomes simply one more step in the inner development which is implied.

It is the Saint herself who now wins victory as, "lifted up in the air," she tramples her foe, singing hymns as she does so. She is thrown into a state of enthusiasm, an ecstatic condition in which she sings hymns as a means of banishing her doubts—which are embodied in the Egyptian. Praising God meant at the same time making a mental sacrifice *(thysia logike)* for the purpose of receiving the divine help. It was really a means of fighting. In this connection, Clement of Alexandria says:

> Out of Zion shall go forth the law, and the word of the Lord from Jerusalem, the heavenly word, a true fighter crowned in the theater of the whole cosmos.[93]

Ecstatic prophesying played a particularly important role among the Montanists. Montanus even once said of himself:

> Behold, man is like a lyre and I myself play on it as the plectron [being himself the Paraclete]. Man is asleep, but I am awake.[94]

It is interesting that the Montanist prophetess Maximilla should also have said of herself: "I am the word, *pneuma* and *dynamis.* "[95]

---

[93] *Protreptikos,* 1. 3.

[94] See Epiphanius, *Panarion,* 48. 4.

[95] Kirsopp Lake, *The Ecclesiastical History with an English Translation,* p. 26.

Thus, Perpetua also becomes the pure Logos (hence her masculinity). In this way she overcomes the spirit of doubt and attains the living, unquestionable faith, symbolized in the bough which the *lanista* presents to her with a kiss. This is the kiss of peace, which was a custom in the early Church; the kiss of life, of which the twenty-eighth ode in *Odes of Solomon* says: "Immortal life has come forth and has kissed me, and from that life is the Spirit within me, and it cannot die, for it lives."[96]

As the outer destruction draws nearer, the comforting images in Perpetua's dreams increase. It is also doubtless owing to the general compensatory function of the unconscious that it was particularly the martyrs in prison and the monks who gave themselves up to a life of asceticism in the desert who enjoyed frequent dreams of wonderful banquets and beautiful heavenly gardens.

The terrible events actually connected with the martyrdom of Perpetua and her fellow-sufferers parallel the dream images. They are their outer fulfillment and, at the same, their denial. As Saturus takes the lead in the dream, so he is the first to be put to death; as Perpetua lays aside her garment in the dream, so the mad cow tears her dress to shreds, exposing her nakedness; and just as the Egyptian threatens to pierce her with his sword, so she is actually pierced by the sword of the gladiator (and this contrary to all expectation, thanks to the intercession of the crowd on her behalf).

Therefore, one might even say that in outer reality the Egyptian conquered. But his triumph was like the victory of Hell and death when Christ was crucified. Through suffering these, Christ remained victorious.[97] Thus, in a certain sense, Perpetua suffers the very fate of Christ; in the words of St. Paul, "Christ" is "formed in" her (Gal. 4:19). Because consciously she is entirely on the side of one of the

---

[96] Bernard, *Odes of Solomon,* ode 28. Literally, "for it is life itself."
[97] "Death is swallowed up in victory. O death, where is thy sting? O grave, where is thy victory?" (1 Cor. 15:54-55)

pairs of opposites in the unconscious and becomes identical with it, the other appears as her outer fate. Yet the very fact of being torn by the conflict (whose truest symbol is the cross of Christ) also offers the possibility of a new life (alluded to in the vision as the bough with the golden apples).

When the deepest layers of the collective unconscious are stirred, as they were at that time, with an emerging new symbol of God, outer events also seem to take part in the process—miracles come to pass. For instance, when the martyrs were put to death, incidents occurred whose unconscious logical sequence seems hardly credible to rational consciousness: not only did the Egyptian apparently conquer with his sword, but also at first it was even decided by the organizers of the games that the women martyrs should appear in white robes, as priestesses of Ceres, and the men, in scarlet, as priests of Saturn.

The martyrs protested on the grounds that they gave their lives precisely to avoid having to do anything of the kind. The suggestion was finally dropped. It was, in fact, a widespread custom at that time to make criminals who had been sentenced play such roles in the amphitheater, but the extraordinary thing is the choice of the gods whose priests the martyrs would have to impersonate. The women were to serve Ceres, the greatest Mother-Deity of antiquity, the Earth Mother and Mother of the Corn, the protectress of young women.

It was just this principle, however, that Perpetua and her fellow martyr Felicitas had repudiated. Perpetua forsook her infant son; Felicitas gave birth to a child in prison only shortly before her martyrdom. And what is still more amazing is that they were thrown to a mad cow.

The cow itself is a widespread ancient symbol of the feminine and maternal principle. The author of the "Passio Perpetuae" seems somehow to have sensed the singularity of this coincidence, for he says:

As to the young women, the devil had kept a mad cow in store for them—which had been provided quite exceptionally *[praetor consuetudi-*

*nem]*—in order by means of the animal, to insult their sex still further by aping it *[sexui earum etiam de bestia aemulatus]*.

An equally astonishing coincidence of outer circumstances is to be found concerning the male martyrs. They were to appear as priests of Saturn, and two of them bore names which happen to be derivations of Saturn: one was Saturus, the other Saturninus.

In Africa, the Roman Saturn was identified with a native Punic-Phoenician deity and played a significant role in the cult of the country. In the old inscriptions he is called *frugifer* (fruit-producing) or *deus frugum* (god of fruit) and is compared to Ceres. The cult of this god was exceptionally widespread in Africa, as the apologetic writings of Tertullian show.[98] In a list of bishops recorded by Cyprian (Epist. 557), no fewer than four bear the name Saturninus. According to Tertullian, the priests of Saturn had particularly broad purple stripes on their togas, also a loose garment in Galatian red.[99] So they wore exactly the same clothing as the gigantic *lanista* in Perpetua's vision—evidence yet again of the bewildering similarity of the opposites.

Saturday was the day consecrated to Saturn and it also coincided with the Sabbath of the Jews, so it was believed at the time that Saturn was the highest god of the Jews. Since no distinction was generally made between Christians and Jews, he was also thought of as the God of the Christians. So the idea which occurred to the organizers of the games—to dress up the martyrs specifically as priests of Saturn—undoubtedly had its origin in these connections.

Thus the law of the enantiodromia of all archetypal opposites fulfilled itself in the martyrs up to the bitter end, and the tension of the wrenching apart of those opposites produced a new life-energy with which the Christian culture of the following centuries was to build

---

[98] See Franz Joseph Dölger, *Ichthys*, vol. 2, pp. 277ff.

[99] *De Pallio*, 4. [For English, see Roberts and Donaldson, eds., *Ante-Nicene Fathers*, vol. 3.—Ed.]

afresh. But the unconscious itself sustained the martyrs with images which held the promise of new life, thereby giving them the inner strength to stand unwaveringly by their decision.

These visions of the "Passio Perpetuae" therefore reveal in a singularly complete form the whole unconscious situation of humanity at that time, pagan as well as Christian. They also show the conflict the Christians experienced in endeavoring to tear themselves free from the spirit which was bound up in nature and in matter. Martyrdom itself had indeed no other meaning than to demonstrate to the pagan world this complete separation and the absolute belief in a world beyond. But the visions also show what hard battles the believers had to fight within themselves, how deep the inner struggle, which in reality had broken out between two divine, suprapersonal unconscious powers.

In truth, viewed psychologically, the martyrs can be seen as tragic, unconscious victims of the transformation which was then being fulfilled deep down in the collective stratum of the human soul. This was the transformation of the image of God, whose new form was to rule over the aeons to come.

Figure 8. Chapel dedicated to St. Perpetua.
(National Shrine of the Little Flower Catholic Church,
Royal Oak, Michigan)

# Appendix
## Saturus's Vision

We had died and had put off the flesh, and we began to be carried towards the east by four angels who did not touch us with their hand. But we moved along not on our backs facing upwards but as though we were climbing up a gentle hill. And when we were free of the world, we first saw an interior light. And I said to Perpetua (for she was at my side): "This is what the Lord promised us. We have received his promise."

While we were being carried by these four angels, a great open space appeared, which seemed to be a garden, with rose bushes and all manner of flowers. The trees were as tall as cypresses, and their leaves were constantly falling. In the garden there were four other angels more splendid than the others. When they saw us they paid us homage and said to the other angels in admiration: "Why, they are here! They are here!"

Then the four angels that were carrying us grew fearful and set us down. Then we walked across to an open area by way of a broad road, and there we met Jucundus, Saturninus, and Artaxius, who were burnt alive in the same persecution, together with Quintus who had actually died as a martyr in prison. We asked them where they had been. And the other angels said to us: "First come and enter and greet the Lord."

Then we came to a place whose walls seemed to be constructed of light. And in front of the gate stood four angels, who entered in and put on white robes. We also entered and we heard the sound of voices in unison chanting endlessly: "Holy, Holy, Holy!" In the same place we seemed to see an aged man with white hair and a youthful face, though we did not see his feet. On his right and left were four elders, and behind them stood other aged men. Surprised, we entered and stood before a throne: four angels lifted us up and we kissed the aged man and he touched our faces with his hand. And the elders said to us: "Let us rise." And we rose and gave the kiss of peace. Then the elder said to us: "Go and play." To Perpetua I said: "Your wish is granted." She said to me: "Thanks be to God that I am happier here now than I was in the flesh."

Then we went out and before the gates we saw the bishop Optatus on the right and Aspesius the presbyter and teacher on the left, each of them far apart and in sorrow. They threw themselves at our feet and said: "Make peace between us. For you have gone away and left us thus." And we said to them: "Are you not our bishop, and are you not our presbyter? How can you fall at our feet?" We were very moved and embraced them.

Perpetua then began to speak with them in Greek, and we drew them apart into the garden under a rose arbour. While we were talking with them, the angel said to them: "Allow them to rest. Settle whatever quarrels you have among yourselves." And they were put to confusion. Then they said to Optatus: "You must scold your flock. They approach you as though they had come from the games, quarrelling about the different teams."

And it seemed as though they wanted to close the gates. And there we began to recognize many of our brethren, martyrs among them. All of us were sustained by a most delicious odour that seemed to satisfy us. And then I woke up happy.[100]

---

[100] Musurillo, trans., "Perpetua," in *Acts of the Christian Martyrs,* pp. 119ff.

# Bibliography

Adlington, W., trans. *The Golden Ass of Apuleius* (1566). New York: Modern Library, 1932.

Bernard, J.H., ed. *The Odes of Solomon.* In J.A. Robinson, *Texts and Studies: Contributions to Biblical and Patristic Literature.* Cambridge: Cambridge University Press, 1891.

Berthelot, M. *Collection des Anciens Alchemistes Grecs.* Paris: Ministry of Public Information, 1887.

Betz, Hans Dieter, ed. *The Greek Magical Papyri in Translation: Including the Demotic Spells.* Chicago: University of Chicago Press, 1992.

Cabrol, Fermand, ed. *Dictionnaire d'Archéologie Chrétienne et de Liturgie.* Paris: Letouzey et Ané, 1907.

Cavalieri, P. Franchi de. *La Passio SS. Perpetuae et Felicitatis.* Rome, 1896.

Colson, F.H., and Whitaker, G.H., eds. *Philo with an English Translation.* New York: Putnam's, 1929.

Cumont, F. *Textes et monuments figurés relatifs aux mystères de Mithra,* Brussels: H. Lamertin, 1896-99.

Dieterich, A. *Nekyia.* Leipzig, 1893.

Dölger, Franz Josef. *Antike Parallelen zum Leidenden Dinocrates in der Passio Perpetuae, Antike und Christentum.* Münster, 1930.

_____. *Ichthys,* vol. 2. Münster, n.d.

Dronke, Peter. *Women Writers of the Middle Ages: A Critical Study of Texts from Perpetua to Marguerite Porete.* Cambridge: Cambridge University Press, 1984.

Edinger, Edward F. *The Aion Lectures: Exploring the Self in C.G. Jung's* Aion. Toronto: Inner City Books, 1996.

_____. *The Psyche in Antiquity, Book 2: Gnosticism and Early Christianity.* Toronto: Inner City Books, 1999.

James, M.R., ed. *Two Lectures on the Newly Discovered Fragments, etc.* 2nd ed. London: 1892.

Jung, C.G. *The Collected Works* (Bollingen Series XX). 20 vols. Trans. R.F.C. Hull. Ed. H. Read, M. Fordham, G. Adler, Wm. McGuire. Princeton: Princeton University Press, 1953-1979.

Jung, Emma. *Animus and Anima.* Zurich: Spring Publications, 1978.

Kerényi, K., and Jung, C.G. *Essays on a Science of Mythology.* Princeton: Princeton University Press, 1969.

King, Charles William *The Gnostics and Their Remains: Ancient and Medieval.* London, 1864.

Labriolle, Pierre de. *La Crise Montaniste.* Paris: Ernest Leroux, 1913.

Lake, Kirsopp. *The Ecclesiastical History with an English Translation.* New York: Putnam's, 1926-32.

Landesdörfer, P.S., ed. *Ausgewählte Schriften der syrischen Dichter.* Kempsten, 1913.

Migne, Jacques Paul, ed. *Patrologiae cursus completus.* Latin series: 221 vols., Paris, 1844-64. Greek series: 166 vols., Paris, 1857-66.

Morfill, W.R., ed., and Charles, R.H., trans. *The Book of the Secrets of Enoch* (1896). Escondido, CA: Book Tree, 1999.

Muncey, R. Waterville. *The Passion of Perpetua: An English Translation with Introduction and Notes.* London: J.M. Dent, 1927.

Musurillo, Herbert, trans. *The Acts of the Christian Martyrs.* Oxford: Oxford University Press, 1972.

Owen, E.C.E. *Some Authentic Acts of Early Martyrs.* Oxford: Oxford University Press, 1927.

Preisendanz, Karl L., ed. *Papyri Magicae Graecae.* Leipzig: B.G. Teubner, 1928.

Rahner, Hugo. "Antemna Crucis II." In *Zeitschrift für Katholische Theologie,* 1942.

Reitzenstein, Richard. *Hellenistische Mysterienreligionen.* Leipzig: B.G. Teubner, 1908. [English: *Hellenistic Mystery Religions: Their Basic Ideas and Significance.* Trans. J.E. Steely. Pittsburgh: Pickwick Press, 1978.]

_____. *Hellenistische Wunderzählungen.* Leipzig: B.G. Teubner, 1906.

_____. *Poimandres.* Leipzig: B.G. Teubner, 1904.

Roberts, A., and Donaldson, J., eds. *The Ante-Nicene Fathers: Translations of the Writings of the Fathers Down to A.D. 325.* Grand Rapids, MI: Wm. B. Eerdmans Publishing Co., 1986.

Robinson, J.A. *Texts and Studies: Contributions to Biblical and Patristic Literature.* Cambridge: Cambridge University Press, 1891.

Salisbury, Joyce E. *Perpetua's Passion: The Death and Memory of a Young Roman Woman.* New York: Routledge, 1997.

Scott, W., ed. *Hermetica.* Oxford University Press, Oxford, 1924.

Shewring, W.H. *The Passion of SS. Perpetua and Felicity.* London: Sheed and Ward, 1931.

*Theatrum Chemicum.* 6 vols. Ursell and Strasbourg, 1602-61.

van Beek, C.J.M.J. *Passio Sanctarum Perpetuae et Felicitatis.* Vol. 1 of *Textum Graecum et Latinum ad Fidem Codicum MSS.* Nijmegen, 1956.

Wilhelm, Richard, trans. *The I Ching or Book of Changes.* London: Routledge and Kegan Paul, 1968.

Zimmermann, Joh. J. *Disquisitiones Historicae et Theologicae, de Visionibus.* Tiguri, 1738.

# Index

Entries in *italics* refer to illustrations

# Also by Marie-Louise von Franz in this Series

### ANIMUS AND ANIMA IN FAIRY TALES
ISBN 1-894574-01-X. (2002) 128pp. *Sewn* $16

Dr. von Fanz devoted much of her life to the difficult task of interpreting fairy tales. Here she focuses on what they can tell us about the contrasexual complexes—animus and anima—that inform our fantasies and behavior concerning the opposite sex, both inner and outer.

### AURORA CONSURGENS
**On the Problem of Opposites in Alchemy**
ISBN 0-919123-90-2. **Hard cover** (2000) 576pp. *Sewn* $40

A penetrating commentary on a rare medieval treatise, scattered throughout with insights relevant to the individuation of modern men and women. Originally published in 1966 as a companion volume to Jung's *Mysterium Coniunctionis.*

### THE PROBLEM OF THE PUER AETERNUS
ISBN 0-919123-88-0. (2000) 288pp. **11 illustrations** *Sewn* $22

The term *puer aeternus* (Latin, eternal youth) is used in Jungian psychology to describe a certain type of man or woman: charming, creative, and ever in pursuit of elusive dreams. This is the classic study of those who remain adolescent well into their adult years.

### THE CAT
**A Tale of Feminine Redemption**
ISBN 0-919123-84-8. (1999) 128pp. **8 illustrations** *Sewn* $16

"The Cat" is a Romanian fairy tale about a princess who at the age of seventeen is bewitched—turned into a cat. . . . One by one von Franz unravels the symbolic threads in this story, from enchantment to beating, the ringing of bells, golden apples, somersaults, witches, etc., and, throughout, the great themes of redemption and the union of opposites.

**C.G. JUNG**
**His Myth in Our Time**
ISBN 0-919123-78-3. (1998) 368pp. **30-page Index** *Sewn* $25
The most authoritative biography of Jung, comprising an historical account of his seminal ideas, including his views on the collective unconscious, archetypes and complexes, typology, creativity, active imagination and individuation.

**ARCHETYPAL PATTERNS IN FAIRY TALES**
ISBN 0-919123-77-5. (1997) 192pp. *Sewn* $20
In-depth studies of six fairy tales—from Spain, Denmark, China, France and Africa, and one from the Grimm collection—with references to parallel themes in many others.

**REDEMPTION MOTIFS IN FAIRY TALES**
**The Psychological Meaning**
ISBN 0-919123-01-5. (1980) 128pp. *Sewn* $16
A nonlinear approach to the significance of fairy tales for an understanding of the process of psychological development. Concise explanations of complexes, projection, archetypes and active imagination. A modern classic.

**ON DIVINATION AND SYNCHRONICITY**
**The Psychology of Meaningful Chance**
ISBN 0-919123-02-3. (1980) 128pp. **15 illustrations** *Sewn* $16
A penetrating study of the psychological aspects of time, number and methods of divining fate such as the I Ching, astrology, Tarot, palmistry, dice, etc. Extends and amplifies Jung's work on synchronicity, contrasting Western attitudes with those of the East.

**ALCHEMY**
**An Introduction to the Symbolism and the Psychology**
ISBN 0-919123-04-X. (1980) 288pp. **84 illustrations** *Sewn* $22
Designed as an introduction to Jung's weighty writings on alchemy. Invaluable for interpreting images in modern dreams and for an understanding of relationships. Rich in insights from over 30 years of analytic practice.

# Studies in Jungian Psychology
# by Jungian Analysts

*Quality Paperbacks*

*Prices and payment in $US (except in Canada, $Cdn)*

**Creating a Life: Finding Your Individual Path**
*James Hollis (Houston)* ISBN 0-919123-93-7. 160 pp. $18

**Jung and Yoga: The Psyche-Body Connection**
*Judith Harris (London, Ontario)* ISBN 0-919123-95-3. 160 pp. $18

**Jungian Psychology Unplugged: My Life as an Elephant**
*Daryl Sharp (Toronto)* ISBN 0-919123-81-3. 160 pp. $18

**Conscious Femininity: Interviews with Marion Woodman**
*Introduction by Marion Woodman (Toronto)* ISBN 0-919123-59-7. 160 pp. $18

**The Middle Passage: From Misery to Meaning in Midlife**
*James Hollis (Houston)* ISBN 0-919123-60-0. 128 pp. $16

**Eros and Pathos: Shades of Love and Suffering**
*Aldo Carotenuto (Rome)* ISBN 0-919123-39-2. 144 pp. $18

**Descent to the Goddess: A Way of Initiation for Women**
*Sylvia Brinton Perera (New York)* ISBN 0-919123-05-8. 112 pp. $16

**Addiction to Perfection: The Still Unravished Bride**
*Marion Woodman (Toronto)* ISBN 0-919123-11-2. Illustrated. 208 pp. $20pb/$25hc

**The Illness That We Are: A Jungian Critique of Christianity**
*John P. Dourley (Ottawa)* ISBN 0-919123-16-3. 128 pp. $16

**Coming To Age: The Croning Years and Late-Life Transformation**
*Jane R. Prétat (Providence)* ISBN 0-919123-63-5. 144 pp. $18

**Jungian Dream Interpretation: A Handbook of Theory and Practice**
*James A. Hall, M.D. (Dallas)* ISBN 0-919123-12-0. 128 pp. $16

**Phallos: Sacred Image of the Masculine**
*Eugene Monick (Scranton)* ISBN 0-919123-26-0. 30 illustrations. 144 pp. $18

**The Sacred Prostitute: Eternal Aspect of the Feminine**
*Nancy Qualls-Corbett (Birmingham)* ISBN 0-919123-31-7. 20 illustrations. 176 pp. $20

**Personality Types: Jung's Model of Typology**
*Daryl Sharp (Toronto)* ISBN 0-919123-30-9. 128 pp. $16

**The Eden Project: In Search of the Magical Other**
*James Hollis (Houston)* ISBN 0-919123-80-5. 160 pp. $18

*Discounts: any 3-5 books, 10%; 6-9 books, 20%; 10 or more, 25%*

*Add Postage/Handling: 1-2 books, $6 surface ($10 air); 3-4 books, $8 surface ($12 air);*
  *5-9 books, $15 surface ($20 air); 10 or more, $10 surface ($25 air)*

Ask for **Jung at Heart** newsletter and free Catalogue of **over 100 titles**

INNER CITY BOOKS
Box 1271, Station Q, Toronto, ON M4T 2P4, Canada

Tel. (416) 927-0355  /  Fax (416) 924-1814  /  E-mail: sales@innercitybooks.net